Kathy

DREAM
BiG !

Ed Green

PRAISE FOR
SHINE YOUR LIGHT

"In *SHINE YOUR LIGHT: Navigate Your Way to a Life You Love*, Ed Gerety brilliantly weaves together thoughtful insights, heartfelt stories and practical ideas to navigate life's challenges through any trial or tribulation. In his clear, compelling and straightforward way, the author invites the reader to consider life in a renewed way filled with peace, joy and compassion. Ed brings to his writing his deep roots in the world of leadership and education peppered with real stories that will touch the heart of readers. A book for young and old!"

—**Julianne Stanz**, Author of *Braving the Thin Places*

"Ed Gerety's *Shine Your Light* delivers on its promise to help readers everywhere navigate our way to a life we will love. With anecdotes, stories, and solid strategies that we can all implement, Gerety demonstrates how resilience, courage, respect, kindness, and gratitude give us all the light we need to get safely to shore. Drawing on sources from Maya Angelou to Taylor Swift, *Shine Your Light* gives practical tips on how to change our attitudes and our mindsets to keep our sails set toward our goals and our dreams."

—**Thomas Edwards**, Provost, Thomas College

"Using nautical themes, this book challenges the reader to 'captain their own ship'. There is a lot to love about this book — inspiring quotes, easy to understand concepts, and lists of insightful questions to guide a person to make better decisions. This book made me think...and it will make you think too!"

—**Jon Mattleman**, Mental Health Consultant

"For over two decades, Ed has inspired me to be my best. Every time I hear him speak, I am more committed to my goals and being a better person. Now, with SHINE YOUR LIGHT: Navigate Your Way To A Life You Love, I have Ed's advice and guidance with me at all times. Ed walks us through navigating life's challenges by taking charge—with your mindset and attitude along with setting goals. He combines this with ensuring awareness of our impact on others by being accountable, kind and sharing our gratitude. The result is a navigation aide for life's journeys—whether you are just starting your journey or a few decades in and need a few reminders. Ed will ensure you focus on what is important and ensure you live your best life."

—**Andrew Shepardson**, Dean of Students, Bentley University

"SHINE YOUR LIGHT: Navigate Your Way to a Life You Love is an incredible read for all ages, young and old! It is woven with such riches shared through Ed's experience as an inspirational speaker, as well as stories he shares from people he has met along his journey. These life lessons are filled with love, laughter, and inspiration. Who doesn't need a little more possibility, accountability, kindness, gratitude, and charting of your course - with master storyteller, Ed Gerety, as your guide!"

—**Coleen Thurber**, a Thirty-year Teacher & Recipient:
Life Changer of the Year Award

"This book is a game-changer for student athletes. It's a compass that will not only guide you to success on the field but also help you win at the game of life!"

—**Meghan Root**, Syracuse University Women' Soccer Captain,
Soladay Award Recipient and
NCAA Jim McKay Award Recipient

"Over the past twenty years, I have personally watched Ed Gerety inspire the students, parents and staff of Bedford, NH with his positive, insightful, and charismatic speeches. His captivating presentations are the perfect combination of sage wisdom and practical advice. It gives me great joy to see Ed translate his spoken word into this book. I sincerely hope this book will allow his message to go even farther into the world and inspire more people to embrace their full potential."

—**Ed Joyce**, Principal, Ross A. Lurgio Middle School

"In an era marked by uncertainty and chaos, this book arrives as the perfect companion at precisely the right time. It will guide you through uncharted waters to new heights of success in both your personal and professional life."

—**Justin Jumper**,
Sr. Director - Field Reimbursement - Dermatology

"*SHINE YOUR LIGHT: Navigate Your Way to a Life You Love* is a passionate compilation of stories and guiding principles to help you to become the best leader and version of yourself. The stories shared represent the true nature of the human spirit and allow for us to feel connected and motivated. As someone who is fortunate to have known Ed for many years, I can say that this is a true reflection of his heart and dedication to helping people to dream big and accomplish their goals. I am confident that this book will provide more access to these important life lessons and challenge readers to go further than they think they can, have an attitude of gratitude, and learn how to navigate those rough seas that we all face at some point in our lives."

—**Bobbi-Lynn Kekic**, Executive Director,
Orientation and Student Onboarding, Bentley University

"I've had the privilege of seeing Ed Gerety in action for almost two decades delivering a motivational address to our students as they begin their college career. In this book, Ed has captured what he does in his outstanding presentations on the written pages. A perfect combination of inspiration and practical tips that are sure to help you achieve your goals."

—**Keith Eldridge**, Dean of Students at Lincoln Center,
Fordham University

"The more I read, I felt as if Ed was next to me sharing this story just for me to understand right now in my life as he reminds you to keep your heart and ears open to those who believe in you. You are reminded to celebrate the journey and be grateful to steer your ship toward the horizon. Thank you, Ed, for once again setting reset with your powerful words and stories of life, love and gratitude. A MUST read for your next reflection."

—**Ms. Morgan Tavis**, Smithtown High School East,
Social Studies Department - Leadership Teacher

BE CONFIDENT ♦ ACHIEVE YOUR GOALS ♦ INSPIRE OTHERS

SHINE YOUR LIGHT

Navigate Your Way to a Life You Love

ED GERETY

To the Three Lighthouses in my life
that give me Strength, Joy, and Love:

Suzanne, Ryan, Shannon

ACKNOWLEDGMENTS

My mom and dad will always be my guiding light, watching over me and serving as an example of what truly matters in life.

The courage and resilience to persist every day are personified in my sister, Joanne. Your unwavering support and ability to bring a smile to my face are treasured gifts.

To Mark and Steve, my brothers, thank you for always believing in me and standing up for my greatness. "For the strength of the pack is the wolf, and the strength of the wolf is the pack."

To Kathy Blake, your love and inspiration have always encouraged me to become the best version of myself.

I express deep gratitude to Susan Hobbs, my business manager, collaborator, and confidante. Your steadfast loyalty, generous spirit, and shining light have profoundly impacted me both professionally and personally. Onward and upward, we go!

To my friends, past and present, your influence is a thread that weaves through this book, representing the countless life lessons you have taught me. Thank you for the kindness and grace you've shown me, in good times and bad. You know who you are, and you will forever hold a place in my heart.

To my mentors and teachers who have continually inspired me to keep moving forward: You've been instrumental in my development as an entrepreneur, speaker, and author. Thank you for opening so many doors and shining a light on the realm of possibilities. You are the giants in my life, represented by your remarkable wisdom and guidance. You continue to inspire and profoundly influence me.

To Alena Ciriello, your guidance, wisdom, and steadfast support have been instrumental in shaping my journey.

To Tracy, Jean, and the Exeter Power Yoga community - The sense of community you foster is truly inspiring. You are an important part in my personal and spiritual growth. Namaste.

Pam and Bart: I am incredibly fortunate to have your commitment to my health and wellness.

Denise McGrath, thank you for being a positive force and uplifting spirit in my life.

To the students and leaders I have had the privilege to speak to at your schools, events, and conferences, and to everyone who contributed to the stories in this book: thank you for your spirit, vulnerability, and courage. I am humbled and inspired by your resilience, hope, and compassion. Keep shining your light!

CONTENTS

INTRODUCTION

"O Captain! My Captain!"
—WALT WHITMAN

I had always dreamed of having a boat and taking it out on the ocean. However, with two little kids and a calendar already full of activities and responsibilities, it didn't seem possible. Not to mention the fact that not only had I never owned a boat before, but I also had never driven one, especially on the ocean.

That quickly changed when my friend Dave introduced me to a company called the Freedom Boat Club. There, members enjoy unlimited use of 40 boats at their various marinas along the seacoast. It seemed to be the perfect solution to making my dream come true. I wouldn't have to worry about maintenance, storage, cleaning, and the other time-consuming and costly issues of owning a boat.

All I had to do was get my boating license, take a quick lesson on the water, and I would be all set. The ironic thing about getting my boating license was that most of the instruction happened in a classroom, not on the water. The one lesson on the water was mostly about how to start the boat and where to find the life jackets in case of an emergency.

Once licensed, I was full of excitement as I was now officially the "captain" of my boat. So when the opportunity came along to take my family on a boat ride along the seacoast on a beautiful morning in July, I jumped at the chance. On the boat that morning was my wife, Suzanne; our two kids, Ryan and Shannon, my mother-in law, Kathy; and her partner, Stan. I was driving a beautiful 28-foot Chaparral sport boat with red trim.

Everything was going great until I had to drive the boat into a marina to get gas. I was having a difficult time adjusting to the strong currents and waves as I pulled near the filling station. I started to get frustrated and overwhelmed as I couldn't get the boat to the gas dock, no matter how hard I tried.

Kathy stepped in and suggested that Stan, who had been in the Navy and had a boat his whole life, should drive. After Kathy repeated this suggestion several times, I defeatedly handed over the keys.

Unfortunately, Stan had not driven a boat in several years. and he wasn't familiar with that type of boat or the marina we were in. As you might guess, things quickly took a turn for the worse. As he shifted gears, he accidentally slammed the throttle in full reverse, and the boat started speeding backward toward a 65-foot lobster boat that was moored in its dock. I thought it was the end for me and my family. But at the last second, I pulled the keys from the ignition, and the boat stalled just inches away from what could have been a devastating crash.

This terrifying moment taught me one of life's most important lessons: When it comes to navigating your life, there can only be one captain, and that captain is you!

You are 100% responsible for your life and in charge of your own journey. If you give that power away, it can put not only you, but also your loved ones at risk. In our fast-paced, hyper-connected world, it's easy to feel lost and uncertain about your path. I know that during difficult times in my life I've felt adrift in a vast and unpredictable sea, with no clear direction or purpose. Maybe you can relate? Are there challenges and obstacles you're dealing with in your life right now that are making you feel discouraged and overwhelmed? Do you know where you're going or how you'll get there?

One of my favorite landmarks on the ocean is a lighthouse. I've always been inspired by how its beacon of light shines out into the darkness to guide ships safely to shore. It's consistently been a symbol to me of strength, power, and hope.

In this book, I'm going to give you five lighthouses to help you chart your course, navigate life's challenges, and shine your light for others to follow. They will guide you toward more gratitude for the gifts in your life and more resilience in the face of adversity. These lighthouses will help you navigate the seas of life with more confidence, freedom, and peace. "O Captain! My Captain!" let the journey begin.

Setting Sail

*"If one advances confidently
in the direction of [their] dreams,
and endeavors to live the life which [they] have imagined,
[they] will meet with a success
unexpected in common hours."*

—HENRY DAVID THOREAU

BEYOND THE HORIZON

"The same wind blows on us all;
the difference in arrival is not the blowing of the wind,
but the set of the sail."

—JIM ROHN

"Can I really finish? Am I strong enough? How can I go any farther? Maybe I should stop." These were the questions racing through my mind at the 20.5-mile mark of the Boston Marathon, the world's oldest annual marathon and one of the world's most prestigious running events. I was at the final hill, infamously known as Heartbreak Hill. For many runners, that is where the dream of completing this marathon ends and hearts are broken. It's the toughest stretch on the course because it not only punishes your legs, but also challenges you mind.

At that moment, my mind was being overtaken by self-doubt and negative thoughts. I knew I had to change my attitude and mindset if I were going to keep moving forward and finish the race.

So I started to answer the questions that were slowing me down with positive statements. "I will finish this race because I have trained hard for more than a year. I have put the miles in and fueled my body with healthy foods. I can go farther than I think I can. Keep going! You're doing a great job! One step at a time. Listen to the crowd cheering you on. You can do it!"

It took me 4 hours, 12 minutes, and 36 seconds to complete that 26.2-mile marathon. I knew that a key factor in achieving that goal and turning a possible heartbreak into a moment of triumph was choosing my attitude and mindset.

The attitude and mindset you choose influence your power to adapt to change and overcome obstacles in life.

Those challenges that you face are just like the weather—you can't control them, but you can choose how you respond to them. Imagine you're out on a boat in the middle of the ocean. You're sailing along, enjoying the smooth seas and sunshine, when suddenly a storm rolls in. The wind picks up, the waves start crashing against the boat, and the rain starts pouring down. You have a choice: You can complain about the storm and blame the weather for ruining your day, or you can put on your rain jacket, secure the boat, and ride out the storm. In the same way, when you face challenges in life, you can complain and blame others for your problems, or you can choose to put on your "rain jacket" and approach the situation with a positive attitude and winning mindset, reminding yourself that you can go further than you think you can.

One leader who demonstrated the power of a positive attitude and mindset was Nelson Mandela. Despite enduring 27 years of imprisonment during his fight against apartheid in South Africa, Mandela never lost his resolve and belief in the power of forgiveness and reconciliation. His unwavering determination and commitment fueled his efforts to dismantle apartheid and create a society based on equality and freedom. Following his release from prison, Mandela continued to embody a positive spirit and inner strength. He led negotiations that resulted in the peaceful transition from apartheid to democracy, promoting forgiveness and unity among diverse racial and ethnic groups. Nelson Mandela's example demonstrates the power of resilience, overcoming obstacles, and maintaining a positive mindset.

Your attitude and mindset, like Mandela's, can guide you beyond your limitations and towards a new horizon—it's your choice.

BE ON THE LOOKOUT

"Beware the stories you read or tell;
subtly, at night, beneath the waters of consciousness,
they are altering your world."

—BEN OKRI

As the captain of your boat, you need to be on the lookout for any dangers that might lead to collisions with other boats, objects, or even people in the water. Similarly, to protect your attitude and mindset from negativity, you need to maintain that same awareness and vigilance—because the world around you will influence your attitudes and beliefs without your even realizing it.

An easy way to understand this is by looking at how a word or phrase becomes popular among your friends, and, before you know it, it seems like everyone is using it. For example, I started to notice that every time I would ask my teenager a question that they normally would have answered with a simple "Yes," instead their response was "For sure, 100%."

In conversations with their friends, I noticed they would use the same response. Then one day someone asked me a question, and, without even thinking about it, I responded, "For sure, 100%."

Do you remember word games in which you would answer a question after you repeated a word that influenced your thinking? For example, "Say 'white' three times. What do cows drink?" Many people automatically answer "Milk," even though cows drink water. How about "Say 'top' three times. What do you do at a green light?" Did you want to reply "Stop"?

Your attitude and mindset are similar. They are influenced by whom and what you surround yourself with and what you are frequently exposed to. All your senses—touch, hearing, sight, smell, and taste—play a major part in your ability to build and maintain a positive attitude and winning mindset. If you're unaware of that, it can inadvertently affect your outlook in a negative way.

One morning, I felt fantastic as I hopped into my car, only then to hear all the bad news on the radio. As the doom and gloom soaked in, I started feeling stressed and agitated, and my happiness vanished. It dawned on me that being unaware of what I listened to or watched could drastically affect my mood, behavior, and well-being. On other occasions, social media conversations or videos left me feeling upset or not good enough. Today, social science researchers know that constantly being online can trigger anxiety and stress, especially if you feel like you're missing out on key moments. It's important to stay mindful of what you allow into your mind and how it impacts you. By choosing positivity and being intentional about what you listen to or watch, you can protect your peace and nurture your well-being. Remember, it's not just about disconnecting; it's about consciously choosing what you connect to.

As a student in college, I loved reading books that inspired me to follow my dreams and be a force for good in the world. This interest fueled my ambition to become an author and inspirational speaker, as I felt compelled to share my own experiences and insights with others to help them grow and achieve their own goals. Inspiring and uplifting others through my words and stories was a dream that I was determined to pursue.

Despite my age, being in college, and lacking any formal business experience, I decided to do just that and start my own business as a professional speaker and leadership trainer. At first, I faced a lot of skepticism and doubt from those around me. Many people told me I was too young and inexperienced to succeed. However, I refused to let this negativity hold me back. Instead, I focused on the support and encouragement I received from those who *did* believe in me, which included my family, coaches, teachers, and close friends. Over time, my hard work and focusing on the positive paid off. My business grew, and I became a sought-after inspirational speaker and leadership trainer. I even wrote a book about helping others to become inspired, achieve their goals, and make a difference.

Just as a lighthouse stands tall and proud, you also must stand up for your own greatness and the greatness of others. Don't let negativity, pessimism, and the storms of life knock you down or make you forget your self-worth. You must keep shining your light and inspiring others to do the same.

Choose the Right Crew

"The quality of your life is in direct proportion to the quality of the people you choose to surround yourself with.
—TONY ROBBINS

Similar to selecting the right crew members for your boat, it is important to be careful and thoughtful about the people you choose to surround yourself with. Negative or toxic people drain your energy, hurt your self-esteem, and hold you back from achieving your goals. On the other hand, positive, supportive, and like-minded individuals provide encouragement, motivation, and inspiration, and help you reach your full potential. The company you keep has a tremendous influence on your ability to build and strengthen your positive attitude and mindset.

My friend Elena is one of those people who helped me navigate a difficult time when my life was out of balance. I was feeling overwhelmed with all the traveling I was doing for work, projects I had to complete, and major presentations I needed to deliver. I was losing my enthusiasm for what I was doing, and inspiration was lacking. Elena took the time to really listen and understand what I was going through. She didn't judge me or tell me not to worry about it. She didn't try to fix it, change it, or dismiss it. She simply listened, asked questions, and listened some more until finally I was ready to talk about possible solutions and strategies to get out of the darkness and back into the light.

Everyone has experiences that can make them feel discouraged, sad, left out, alone, anxious, scared, or uncertain. These emotions will start to turn your attitude negative and cause your motivation to decline. How you begin to bounce back from challenging times is by being connected with people who are there to listen, offer insights, and remind you that they have your back.

I'm not referring only to your friends when it comes to surrounding yourself with positive people. It also could be a family member, boss, coach, mentor, or teacher.

Deb Thompson, my high school communications teacher, was someone who influenced my life in a positive way. She was always encouraging me to follow my passion and to break through my fears. Many students in the class were afraid of public speaking, and I was one of them. But Miss Thompson didn't let this fear hold me back. Instead, she challenged me to enter a speech competition in my junior year. Despite my nervousness, I took up Miss Thompson's challenge and worked hard to prepare for the competition. Along the way, she provided invaluable guidance and lessons about public speaking and how to communicate effectively. Her encouragement and support gave me the confidence to do my best, and I ended up placing high in the competition. Her positive attitude and love for teaching influenced my professional speaking career. Ultimately, that has resulted in me speaking to more than 3 million people over the past three decades in all 50 states and across Canada.

Be aware that there are going to be times when you sail into rough waters, and it can be easy to drift toward negative and pessimistic individuals who don't share your same enthusiasm for life. These individuals will slow you down and eventually steer you off course. That's what happened to John, a senior at a high school where I was speaking. He came up to me after an assembly and shared how he remembered when I came to his school when he was a freshman. He explained to me how, back then, he was vice president of his class, played in the school band, and was doing great academically. He even had created a dream board of his goals and aspirations.

John said, "I was doing great, and then, without even realizing it, I started hanging out with people who were more into partying than studying and who thought school was kind of a joke. My grades dropped. I didn't run for class office again, and I decided to quit the band. Listening to you today reminded me just how much influence the company we keep can have on the choices and decisions we make." The good news is that John is now learning from his mistakes. He's back on the path to achieving his goals and living his best life with people who are supporting him along the way.

If you don't have the right crew in your life, then it's time to go find them. You can meet new people by getting involved in clubs, activities, or hobbies that interest you. You could join a church, find a civic or volunteer group, or participate in special events in your community. These all provide opportunities to make new connections and friendships.

One of my favorite movies growing up was *Star Wars Episode V: The Empire Strikes Back*. In the movie, Darth Vader tries to convince Luke Skywalker to come to the Dark Side so that together they can rule the galaxy. Luke is tempted, but ultimately he has the courage to say no and walk away. He does this by trusting his inner voice and relying on the wisdom he learned from his teacher, Yoda, who told him "Once you start down the dark path, forever it will dominate your destiny. Consume you, it will." Everyone has "Darth Vaders" who sometimes show up in their life, individuals who dismiss your ideas, make you feel ignored, or try to make you doubt your talents. It's crucial to steer clear of such individuals and keep your sails set toward your goals and dreams.

There are going to be times when people you go to school with, work with, or even live with are in a space of negativity. I use the words "space of negativity" because every human being at their core has goodness within them and the ability to choose to be in a new space of *positivity*. When others are in that negative space, you must stay vigilant and challenge yourself to not take what they say or do personally. You don't have to prove them wrong, try to change them, or get into an argument with them. In fact, when they're done whining, complaining, and telling you that you can't achieve your dream, you can simply respond with "Thanks for sharing." There really is no comeback to that. Think about it.

Someone says, "I don't like you!" Your response: "Thanks for sharing." A person says, "You can't achieve that goal. You're not good enough or smart enough. You could never get into that college. You can't start your own business …." Whatever the negative comment or observation is, you can simply say, "Thanks for sharing."

I was on an airplane once and the person sitting next to me asked what I did for work. When I told them I was an inspirational speaker and author, they responded sarcastically, "Good luck to you, because people today …" and then went on a 30-second rant filled with resignation and cynicism. When he was done, I looked at him, smiled, and said, "Thanks for sharing." Then I opened my book and began to read. That was the end of the conversation.

There are times you can't simply end a conversation with that statement or even walk away and ignore the person. In those conversations, you still can listen with an open mind and an open heart. You can support and encourage them, but you don't have to take their problems and put them on your shoulders.

Choose your crew members carefully. Are they kind, upbeat, patient, and supportive? Do they believe in your greatness? Do they listen with compassion and empathy? The people you surround yourself with can make all the difference in the world when it comes to achieving your dreams and reaching your full potential. They will help you navigate life's challenges with grace and determination.

CHECK YOUR GPS

"Our environment, the world in which we live and work, is a mirror of our attitudes and expectations."
—EARL NIGHTINGALE

During the COVID-19 pandemic, there were times when I felt like I was lost in a sea of uncertainty and drifting aimlessly. I was feeling frustrated, and I was focusing on things that I had no control over. My motivation was low, and everything felt off-center. Maybe you can relate to a time in your life when your confidence was lacking and it seemed like the rough seas would never calm. One of the strategies that helped me get back on course and change my negative attitude was becoming more aware of my surroundings.

The things you surround yourself with, such as inspirational quotes, books, or artwork, can have a big impact on your mindset and attitude. Creating a positive environment cultivates a winning mindset, builds resilience, and creates a positive outlook toward change and challenges. By surrounding yourself with sources that inspire your creativity and enthusiasm, you can find the motivation needed to keep going forward. Just like you use a GPS to give you the confidence to get to your destination, what you focus on and surround yourself with helps you navigate your way to staying positive and having the right mindset.

As a teenager, tennis player Serena Williams posted pictures of the championships she dreamed of winning on her bedroom wall. Today she has won them all and is considered one of the greatest athletes ever to have played the game. American singer-songwriter Taylor Swift has shared in interviews that she is constantly listening to music that inspires her to create new songs and performances. She has sold more than 200 million records globally and is one of the best-selling musicians of all time. Misty Copeland became the first black female principal ballerina in the American Ballet Theatre's

75-year history. She is one of the most widely known ballerinas in the world today because of her talent, hard work, and perseverance. Copeland also credits her success to reading the biographies of ballerinas who came before her, which inspired her to dream big and never give up.

These are just a few examples of individuals who know that another key to being resilient, embracing change, and achieving your goals is not only *who* you surround yourself with, but also *what* you surround yourself with.

Your environment can give you the energy, inspiration, and space to develop the clarity, focus, and inspiration you need to keep moving forward. It can help you stay inspired as you strive to achieve your goals.

If I walked into an area where you spend a lot of time or looked at a space that you call your own, what would I see? Are some of your favorite quotes and pictures there to remind you of where you want to go, who you want to become, and what you want to achieve? Is there a copy of the book you're reading on personal development? Is your space clean, organized, and set up in a way that makes you feel calm and confident? (Yes, that includes making your bed.) Whether it's your car, office, locker, home, or outdoor space, when things are organized and there's a minimum of clutter, you have more energy, more flow, and fewer distractions.

Think about when you stay in a hotel room on a trip. It's easy to feel good because there is no laundry lying around, the air smells clean, and everything has its place. There is simplicity and order, and the colors in the room are bright, refreshing, and visually appealing. You can bring that same clarity, focus, and energy into your own space. It doesn't have to be only when you're on vacation.

Your environment influences what you think about and what you focus on—and, as a result, what you manifest in your life. In my car, I have pictures of my family, our dog, and a quote that makes me smile. These things remind me of why I do what I do, what my priorities are, and to live each day to its fullest. I also try to make sure that I'm aware of what I'm listening to in the car. Music can cause a strong emotional response in the listener. On the positive side, it can make you feel happy, peaceful, calm, and motivated. It also can make you feel sad, lonely, depressed, or even angry. If you're not listening to music, maybe you're tuned in to a podcast on a subject that interests you, or you are just enjoying some quiet time. The books you read also play an important role in helping you stay motivated.

Growing up, my dad would always remind me of the quote by Charlie "Tremendous" Jones: "You will be the same person in five years as you are today except for the people you meet and the books you read." Taking the time to read books related to the areas of your life you want to improve is essential to your ongoing growth and development. When you were a kid, you didn't necessarily get to choose the people who were in your life or the environment you lived in. However, as you get older, you begin to realize that you can choose the company you keep—your friends, your partners, even where you work and whom you work with. You get to choose what you read and listen to, and whether you're willing to take 100% responsibility for your life. When you do, you live into your dreams and don't let the past or where you come from determine or limit your future.

YOUR WORDS MATTER

"Watch your thoughts, they become words; watch your words, they become actions; watch your actions, they become habits; watch your habits, they become character; watch your character, for it becomes your destiny."

—FRANK OUTLAW

How you talk to yourself and the words you use in speaking with others are another key to developing and maintaining a winning mindset and being confident. To achieve a high level of success in any field, you must have a strong belief in yourself. Research shows that a big step in building and protecting your confidence is choosing your words carefully. This often is referred to as positive self-talk, affirmations, declarations, or self-esteem build-ers. My daughter, Shannon, is an actor, and just before she walks onstage to perform, she says three things to herself: "I'm going to do a great job with my solos. I am in the present moment. I can do this!" She explained to me that when she does this, she starts to feel calmer and more focused, which leads to her doing her best onstage.

Your words help create your reality. Have you ever asked someone how well they did something, and they responded with, "Terrible! Everything went wrong, and I can't do anything right. I'm so dumb." All that negativity creates almost a self-fulfilling prophecy that the same thing will happen again the next time they do that same activity. Those self-defeating words chip away at your confidence and attitude. A more powerful way to answer that question would have been "Today was a challenging day and some things did not go the way I wanted them to, but I will come back stronger next time. I know I have the talent to do this." Being brave, confident, resilient, and positive is not a one-time thing where once you have that feeling, you never lose it. You must create it and reinforce it every day.

Let It Go

Serenity Prayer:
God, grant me the serenity
to accept the things I cannot change,
the courage to change the things I can,
and the wisdom to know the difference.

—REINHOLD NIEBUHR

One of the things that can take you off course and cause you to feel overwhelmed, anxious, and tired is when you focus your energy and attention on things you cannot control. It's a waste of energy and mentally exhausting. When you focus on things you cannot control, you are likely to experience frustration because you cannot change the outcome. This frustration leads to feelings of helplessness and can be a significant source of stress.

I was at an airport once and my flight was delayed because of a big thunderstorm passing through. As I was in line to talk with the ticket agent about making my connection, the person in front of me started yelling at the agent, exclaiming, "Excuse me, but this thunderstorm right now is unacceptable!"

I was next in line, and I asked the ticket agent if it was possible for me to make my connection. She said, "I have no idea. The computers are up and then they're down."

I said, "Okay, there's a Starbucks around the corner. I'm going to get a cup of coffee. Would you like one?"

"No, I'm all set, thank you," she said. So I leaned in, smiled, and said, "Hey look, it's six o'clock in the morning. Besides, the thunderstorm is not your fault." The ticket agent smiled and said, "Okay, Grande Pike Place, one cream, one sugar." I came back with a cup of coffee for her.

An hour later, we started boarding the flight and I took my place in line with all the passengers. I gave my ticket to the agent, the woman for whom I had bought the cup of coffee. She looked up, and with no emotion on her face, she said, "Please step aside, sir." I thought to myself, *Great. I'm in trouble.* She took my ticket and ripped it up. Now I'm thinking, *I'm really in trouble.* She quickly printed out another ticket for me and said, "Here you go. By the way, thanks for the cup of coffee."

"Yeah, no problem," I said. I wondered what that interaction was about as I walked away, and then I looked down at my ticket to see the change. I had been upgraded to first class. I turned around to say thank you, and all she said was, "Keep walking, please." I didn't get the ticket agent a cup of coffee because I thought I might get upgraded to first class. It never crossed my mind. It didn't. Now it does. When I go to the airport now, I buy everyone coffee!

Another time, I was having a celebration at my house. I was so concerned that everyone wouldn't get along that I tried to control every topic of conversation. At the end of the night, I was exhausted and felt like I had connected with no one. I realized that when I try to control the behavior or actions of others, it leads me to feel frustrated, angry, and resentful, which can be detrimental to my well-being.

You and I cannot control the weather, another person's behavior, or flight delays ... and yet, so often you give away your energy, focus, and time to those things. When you do that, it creates unnecessary worry and anxiety that negatively impacts your physical and mental health. When you give your attention to what you cannot control, you give away your power and true self-expression. It takes courage to let go of what you cannot control and focus on the things you can. But when you do, a whole new world of possibilities opens up for you, and your attitude and mindset stay strong.

PRACTICE PRESENCE

*"The present moment is filled with joy and happiness.
If you are attentive, you will see it."*

— THICH NHAT HANH

When you are captain of a ship, it's important to keep your focus on the present moment and the current conditions of the sea. Dwelling on the what-ifs, would'ves, could'ves, and should'ves is like constantly looking back at the wake of the ship instead of looking ahead at the horizon. By doing so, you risk losing sight of the dangers and opportunities that lie ahead. Just as a sailor cannot change the wind or the waves that have already passed, you cannot change the events of the past. However, you can learn from them and adjust your course accordingly. It's important to acknowledge the lessons you've learned from past experiences and use them to make better decisions in the present moment.

When you make statements to yourself like *I wish I had tried out for that team last year. I should have started my own business two years ago. If I could only go back and have one more chance ...*, then you instantly pull yourself out of the present moment and into the past. You and I can't do anything about the past. It happened, and it's over. This does not mean that you forget where you come from or the people and experiences that influenced who you are today. It means the only thing you can do with the past is to acknowledge it for what was or was not, learn lessons from it, and then move on to the present moment.

It's easier said than done, especially in a world where we are tapped into technology and social media channels 24/7. There are endless pictures, videos, and movies that glamorize the past or stir up painful memories.

It's these same social networks that can also push you out of the present and into the future. You see the picture of the house on the beach and say to yourself, *Someday, when I live there, I will be happy.* You see a video of your dream car and say, *Someday, when I have that car, I will be free.*

Companies spend billions of dollars every year on advertising, trying to convince you that your joy, happiness, freedom, and ideal life don't exist now, but they will someday, with their product, service, or person.

There is no someday! Your life is right now, and the only way you can achieve any goal in the future is to start by being in the present moment. Being in the present moment is not a one-time thing, where once you are there, you stay. The pull back to the past and the push into the future are constant, which is why you have to practice being present moment by moment.

That practice starts with being conscious of your breath. You may have seen athletes at some of their biggest moments take a deep breath in and let it out before they start. Say that you're about to do something for the first time that is a little scary. Do you take a deep breath in and out before you do it? When you take control of your breathing, you help calm your body and your brain. As a result, you become more focused and intentional, and you feel less stressed.

Here is a simple mindfulness exercise called "breath awareness" that can help put you in the present moment.

To do this exercise, find a quiet and comfortable place to sit or lie down. Close your eyes and bring your attention to your breath. Notice the sensation of the air moving in and out of your nose or mouth, the rise and fall of your chest or belly, and the feeling of your body expanding and contracting with each breath.

As you focus on your breath, you may notice that your mind starts to wander and become distracted by thoughts, emotions, or sensations. This is normal and expected. When you notice your mind has wandered, gently bring your attention back to your breath without judgment.

Through this process of returning your attention to your breath, you cultivate the skill of mindfulness, which is the ability to be fully present and aware in the moment without getting caught up in thoughts, worries, or distractions.

By using your breath as an anchor for your attention, you can train your mind to stay in the present moment and develop greater awareness, focus, and calmness.

Many world-class performers and leaders have a daily practice of meditation or prayer. They understand that this daily practice puts them in the present moment, where they connect with their spirit, mind, and body. This connection enables them to be more positive, resilient, and happy. By doing the same, you can make the most of the opportunities that lie ahead and navigate any challenges that come your way. "Today is a gift. That is why they call it the present." Breathe.

Find Your True North

*"What you do makes a difference,
and you have to decide what kind of difference
you want to make."*

—JANE GOODALL

One of the key ways to stay inspired and keep your confidence and mindset strong is to know *why* you do what you do. What is your higher purpose? Why are you showing up every day—whether it's work, school, sports, performing arts, or other activities? You must have a bigger reason for doing it than just the day-to-day responsibility of showing up. Just like you use a compass to give you a clear direction on your journey, your higher purpose is the driving force that inspires and motivates you to show up every day with passion and commitment.

If you don't know your purpose, it can lead to a decline in your motivation and enthusiasm. You start to feel exhausted, drained, and worn out. This is what happened to Jamal, who was working extra hours on weekends to make more money. He explained to me that, at first, he was excited to have found a weekend job. However, as time went on, he began to dread going to work on Saturdays and Sundays.

He said, "I started thinking about all of the things I was missing out on and questioned why I was even working so hard." Jamal had lost focus and forgot the main reason he got the extra job in the first place. It was not just to help pay the bills. He told me he was working the extra hours so he could save enough money to buy his own home. It was a dream he'd had ever since he was a little boy.

He shared, "I lived in a small apartment with my mom, and before she passed away, I promised her that when I got older, I would buy my own home." Once Jamal got present again to his why—his higher purpose—his drive and desire to work those weekends came back. Jamal now keeps a picture of his dream home in his wallet and on his refrigerator to remind him of his why.

My friend Colleen Thurber is crystal clear on her why. She was a teacher for 30 years and received the LifeChanger of the Year award, which recognizes educators who are making a significant difference in the lives of students by exemplifying excellence, positive influence, and leadership. She told me, "I believe that one of my students will one day change the world. The fact that I might play a small part in that is something I consider to be a privilege, and it gets me excited to come to work every day."

Why did I choose to start my own business as an inspirational speaker, leadership trainer, and author? Most of us are searching for inspiration and for someone to believe in us. Everyone wants to feel valued and accepted for who they are. If I can inspire and help one person achieve their goals, believe in themselves, be more grateful, and live a life they love, then I know that I made a difference. That's why I do what I do. That's my true north. What's yours?

DON'T GIVE UP

"A winner is somebody who has given their best effort,
who has tried the hardest they possibly can,
who has utilized every ounce of energy and strength
within them to accomplish something.
It doesn't mean that they accomplished it or failed;
it means that they've given it their best.
That's a winner."

—WALTER PAYTON

In school, I heard a folk tale about having a positive attitude called "The Special Frog." Here's how it goes.

One day, three frogs were hopping along at a farm when they came across a big bucket of milk and decided to jump in. They started swimming around, laughing, and having a great time. The frogs got thirsty and started to drink some of the milk. As they continued drinking, they found themselves almost at the bottom of the bucket.

Along came four other frogs that had become curious when they heard all kinds of noise coming from the bucket. They hopped up onto the edge of the bucket to see what was going on. One of the four frogs looked down and yelled, "Hey, you three frogs down there, look how far down you are! You drank all that milk and now you're way down in the bottom. You're not going to be able to get out. You're going to drown!"

The first two frogs in the bucket looked up, heard this, and started panicking while trying to jump out of the bucket. The four mean frogs started yelling, "You are not going to make it! You're going to drown. Give up!"

The third frog in the bucket saw the two other frogs jumping wildly to get out. She could see the four frogs up on the edge, waving their arms and kicking their legs. The third frog then started trying to get out of the bucket.

The four mean frogs were yelling. "You're not going to make it! You're going to drown. Give up!" Sadly, the first two frogs gave up and drowned, believing what the four mean frogs told them.

The third frog was still trying to get out of the bucket, and she was completely out of breath. She looked up to see the four mean frogs still waving their arms and yelling and screaming.

She closed her eyes and said, "I know I can do it!" With one last giant leap, the third frog jumped out of the bucket.

Why did the third frog make it out? Because she was deaf. The whole time the four frogs were yelling and screaming and waving their arms and legs, the third frog, with her positive attitude, looked up and said to herself, "Hey, look at those four frogs up there. They must really want me to get out of the bucket." She thought they were yelling, "Come on, get out of the bucket! You can make it, don't give up! You can do it!"

The key lesson of the story: Turn a deaf ear to people who don't encourage you. Keep your heart and ears open to those who believe in you. A positive attitude is one of the most powerful attributes you can have to believe in yourself and persevere.

Brian, a 25-year-old, shared with me how he made that choice. "My business partner decided to quit as our company started to tread water, and I hit rock bottom as far as my entrepreneurial career went. That's when I realized that I had the most powerful experience ever: failure. The moment when my business partner emailed me to tell me he was quitting, I felt defeated ... I felt like a failure. That's when I took a second to just look around. Guess what? The walls weren't falling down. I was still breathing, and the sun was still shining. In that moment, I realized that failure wasn't all that bad. Instead, I realized that I'm powerful now having experienced that. Failure doesn't scare me anymore. The world goes on, and I choose to push on and pave my own path."

Does being positive mean that you always look on the bright side of things, nothing ever bothers you, and you go through every day happy and feeling great about yourself and everyone around you? Absolutely not. We all have bad days, tough weeks, sometimes even a really challenging year. We are human.

It takes courage to bounce back from those times, learn lessons where you can, and then let them go. Just like the unpredictable winds and currents of the ocean, there will be people and events that try to bring you down and discourage you from reaching your destination. Keep on moving forward and don't give up!

MOVING FORWARD
REFLECTION & ACTION

"*Nothing can stop the person with the right mental attitude from achieving their goal; nothing on earth can help the person with the wrong mental attitude.*"

—THOMAS JEFFERSON

MINDSET AND ATTITUDE ARE A CHOICE. WHAT WILL YOU CHOOSE?

attitude: manner, disposition, feeling, position, etc., with regard to a person or thing; tendency or orientation, especially of the mind

mindset: a person's way of thinking and their opinions

1. What is one of the most powerful choices you can make every day?

2. How can you reframe negative thoughts into more positive ones?

3. Who are five people in your life who have a positive attitude/mindset and what qualities do they have in common?

4. What inspires you?

5. Describe a time when you were resilient and had to persevere to overcome an obstacle or achieve a goal.

6. What are three things in your environment that help you stay positive?

7. Share a quote or lyric from a song or movie that inspires you.

8. What are three affirmations you can make today? (e.g., I am calm, confident, and happy.)

9. When you think about creating the life you want, living a life you love, you envision it as a life filled with _____ .
   (e.g., freedom, peace, creativity, opportunity, family)

10. What is one of your main activities/jobs/responsibilities, and what is your why? What is your higher purpose for doing it?

Oceans of Possibilities

*"We keep moving forward, opening new doors,
and doing new things, because we're curious …
and curiosity keeps leading us down new paths."*

—WALT DISNEY

Be Curious

*"Remember the first word you learned—
the biggest word of all—LOOK.
Everything you need to know is in there somewhere."*
—ROBERT FULGHUM

I had just completed my RYT® 200 (200-hour) yoga teacher training certification when a fellow student introduced me to her partner. She said, "Ed, I would like you to meet my husband. He believes that real men don't do yoga."

I was caught off guard by the statement, but then I simply smiled and said, "Nice to meet you, and thanks for sharing." I understood where he was coming from.

A year earlier, I was making my own excuses, judgments, and assumptions about why I should *not* try to be a yoga instructor. *This will be too hard. I'm too old. I'm not flexible enough. I don't have time. I can't stand on my head or do a Bakasana pose*, I told myself. All the reasons and justifications were covering up the real truth: I was afraid. I was afraid of looking bad, afraid of failing, afraid of not being good enough, and afraid of not doing it right.

Stepping outside your comfort zone is scary and, at times, uncomfortable. However, it's the only way you can truly grow, learn, and live your best life. The practice and process of teaching yoga has taught me to not take things personally, to be in the present moment, and to be curious.

In life, sometimes it's not the circumstances that stop you from achieving your goals, but what you tell yourself you can or cannot do. As Richard Bach wrote, "Argue for your limitations, and sure enough they're yours."

~

Stephanie was a junior in college when she realized that she had been holding herself back out of fear and worry and that she needed to take action if she wanted to make a difference in the world.

She decided to start small. She began volunteering at a local non-profit organization that focused on education and empowerment for underprivileged youth. She found that working with these children was incredibly fulfilling, and it sparked a passion in her for helping others.

As she became more involved with the organization, Stephanie started to take on more responsibilities and leadership roles. She found that she was good at motivating others and inspiring them to take action, and she began to see a clear path for her future.

With newfound confidence and determination, Stephanie decided to take a big risk: She applied for a competitive internship program that would take her to a different part of the country for the summer. She was scared to leave her comfort zone and travel alone, but she knew that this was the next step in her journey.

To her surprise, Stephanie was accepted into the program. She spent the summer working with a team of passionate and driven individuals who were all focused on making a difference in the world. The experience was challenging and rewarding, and Stephanie felt more alive than ever before.

When she returned to college in the fall, she was a changed person. She had a clear sense of purpose and direction, and she was no longer afraid to take risks and pursue her dreams. She continued to volunteer with the non-profit organization and became a mentor for other students who were struggling to find their way.

Years later, Stephanie looked back on this time in her life as a turning point. She realized that it was through her curiosity and willingness to take risks that she was able to find her true passion and make a difference in the world. She encouraged others to do the same, to embrace their curiosity, take risks, and never give up on their dreams.

I remember the answer a 12-year-old gave me when I asked, "What if you don't know what your goals are or where you want to go?" They answered with a shrug of their shoulders, "You just Google it!"

As funny as that answer is, it's also true. We live in an incredible time in history when, in a matter of seconds, you can get on the internet, explore any subject, and learn new things. Be gentle with yourself and trust that if you keep searching and being curious, you will find your way. If you have a clear vision of your future and you decide to change it, that's okay too. The average college student changes their major at least once, and most adults have several different careers during their lives. There are going to be stages in life when you feel stuck and uncertain about what your next step should be. You might even start comparing yourself to others and feel pressured to live a dream that someone else has for you. The biggest mistake you can make in life is to live someone else's goal or dream.

My friend Kim shared with me how her parents always wanted her to be a lawyer. They went so far as to pick the law school she should attend. In her heart, she knew that wasn't what she wanted to do. She told me how agonizing it was to be living a lie and pretending she was on the same page as her parents. "It was only when I finally had the courage to tell them my truth that I felt the freedom for the first time to really be myself and look for new possibilities," she said.

To navigate your way to a life you love, like Kim did, you need to listen to and follow your heart. As Henry David Thoreau wrote, "If [one] does not keep pace with [their] companions, perhaps it is because [they hear] a different drummer. Let [them] step to the music which [they hear], however measured or far away." I understand that the journey can be scary at times and cause you to feel unsure of yourself. It's at these moments when you have to trust yourself and face those moments with courage and determination. When you do that, you open yourself up to oceans of possibilities. By embracing new experiences, you will see things you have never imagined before, meet new people, and live a life of excitement and wonder.

SEE IT, BELIEVE IT, ACHIEVE IT

"May your future be limited only by your dreams!"
—CHRISTA MCAULIFFE

I was 22 years old when I attended a leadership training led by my friend Snowden McFall, an inspirational author and speaker. Snowden was a champion of my work and helped me create the first professional marketing materials for my business. It was at this training that she introduced me to the activity of creating dream boards. You also may have heard dream boards referred to as vision boards, goal maps, roadmaps, or treasure maps.

In this exercise, you create a collage of pictures, words, and other symbols that represent and declare your goals and wishes. This powerful visual representation helps you get clarity and visualize your aspirations.

Often, when I ask people what their goals are or where they want to go, their answer is, "I don't know." Doing this exercise will help you find those answers because themes and patterns will appear on your vision board that you may have been unable to find or articulate. You have the opportunity, for the first time, to really see your dreams and ambitions—and the possibility of them coming true.

Maddie, a high school student, experienced this clarity when she created her first dream board. "The exercise opened my eyes to a new way of approaching challenges and life in general with a positive mindset and attitude," she said. "I have been dreaming about attending the U.S. Air Force Academy since the eighth grade. It didn't seem real until I saw it on my dream board. I'm going to put my dream board in a place where I'll wake up and it's the first thing I see. This is exactly what I needed to get inspired and start my sophomore year off right."

Your dream board can be divided into different areas that are important to you, such as school, activities, career, college, or travel. You should display your board in a place that is highly visible to you as a daily reminder of what you're working toward. My son has his on his bedroom ceiling; my daughter has hers on the back of her door; mine is on my office wall.

I have made a dream board every year since that training. They inspire me to stay focused on my goals and remind me why I am giving my best effort. My previous dream boards have included speaking in all 50 states, running in the Boston Marathon, writing a book, finding my soulmate, and taking vacations. All those dreams have come true.

I've shared this powerful exercise with thousands of individuals and heard many inspiring stories of how making a dream board has positively affected their lives.

Nicole shared her story in an email to me. "I heard you speak at a state student council conference where you talked about creating dream boards. I was so inspired that I decided I was going to make a dream board for myself. There is no doubt in my mind that my dream boards have single-handedly changed my life. Despite many personal obstacles, including depression and unknowingly struggling with ADD for the first 18 years of my life, I was able to use my dream board as motivation to point my life in a new direction. Today, I'm a happier, more successful person thanks to you and your message. I'm currently in college with a double major in advertising and art. Thanks to the leadership skills I developed in high school, by 19 years old I had already landed myself a management position at The Gap. Then, I started my own business on the side doing custom illustration and design work. Now I work as an assistant manager with a different retailer, attend school full time, maintain a 3.5 GPA, have a second job as an art director for an advertising agency, and, on occasion, I sell a piece or two of my art. These are just a few of the more recent accomplishments I'm proud to say I have achieved, all of which have one thing in common: They were all on my dream board!"

Is that it? You just create it, post it, and—ta-da!—your wishes come true? Not exactly. I do believe in the law of attraction—that what you think about you become, and what you focus on in your life you attract. However, as Nicole's story demonstrates, you still have to do the work, put in the practice, build your confidence, and go further than you think you can. Otherwise, your dream board is nothing more than just pretty pictures and words that sound nice.

If you want to get started on your own dream board, see the instructions at the end of this chapter.

I WILL

"The difference between a successful person and others is not a lack of strength, not a lack of knowledge, but rather a lack of will."

—VINCE LOMBARDI

It's important to dream big, but then you must get to work and start to turn those dreams into clear, specific, and measurable goals. If you don't do that, your dream will remain just that: a wish, a hope, a "someday" maybe it will come true. When you get clarity on your goals, you get focus. When you focus, you get confidence, and with confidence, you can be unstoppable. People who write down their goals are more likely to achieve them than people who don't. As you write down your goals, use the following goal-setting formula to help you with clarity and focus, and spell out exactly what you'll need to achieve your goals.

WHAT GOALS DO I WANT TO ACHIEVE?

Examples:

~ I want to get my master's degree.

~ I want to earn better grades.

~ I want to play the guitar.

HOW CAN I MAKE MY GOAL AS SPECIFIC AS POSSIBLE?

Examples:

~ I will receive my master's degree in business in the next two years from the University of New Hampshire.

~ I will get a B average or better in my five subjects this school year.

~ I will learn to play my favorite song on the electric guitar in one month.

WHAT RESOURCES AND SKILLS DO I CURRENTLY HAVE THAT WILL HELP ME REACH MY GOAL?

Examples:

~ I love to learn new things. I can earn my degree online and still work my full-time job.

~ I can go in after school for extra help. I can find a friend who does well in each subject and study with them.

~ I know a lot about music. My friend already plays the guitar. I have a neighbor who gives guitar lessons.

WHAT MINI-GOALS DO I NEED TO SET IN ORDER TO ACHIEVE MY GOALS?

Examples:

~ Find out the application due date for the master's program, then confirm I have the requirements and references needed. Know how much it costs and how I will pay for it.

~ Study for my test on Friday with my classmate. Schedule time to meet with my teachers. Use my school planner to organize my assignments.

~ Sign up for lessons. Buy an electric guitar. Learn the song from my friend who plays the guitar.

ON WHAT DATE WILL I ACCOMPLISH EACH MINI-GOAL?

Examples:

~ My application will be submitted by June 1. I will make my first payment on August 15.

~ Study for my test on Friday with my classmate by Wednesday evening. Schedule time to meet with my teachers by Thursday after school. Use my school planner to organize my assignments by Friday.

~ Sign up for lessons by June 2. Buy an electric guitar by June 7. Learn the song from my friend who plays the guitar by June 30.

ON WHAT DATE WILL I ACHIEVE MY GOAL?

Examples:

~ I will complete my master's degree by May 15 of next year.

~ I will earn a B average or better in my five subjects this school year when grades are sent on June 15.

~ I will begin taking lessons this month and learn to play the song on my electric guitar by June 30.

William attended a program of mine when he was in middle school and shared with me how he used this goal-setting formula to achieve his goal. "You called me up onstage in the eighth grade and asked, 'What is your goal?' I said, 'I will be a four-year varsity basketball player in high school.' Despite the challenges stacked against me, I was determined to achieve this goal. I broke it down into smaller, more manageable steps (mini-goals) and worked hard every day to improve my skills and performance.

"Years later, my hard work and determination paid off. I became a four-year varsity player at my high school and was even selected as the team captain. In my senior year, my team was ranked in the top five in the country and won a championship."

William's story is a great example of how setting goals and working toward them with passion and determination can lead to great achievements. When you believe in yourself and put in the effort required, you can accomplish things you once thought impossible. Set your sights high, work hard toward your goals, and make your dreams a reality.

As you sail on your journey toward your goals, remember it's not just about reaching the final destination—it's about who you become and what you learn along the way. During a speech in which I made this point, an attendee named Laura quickly raised her hand and said, "That doesn't make sense. Put forth your best effort, and whether or not you reach your goal, it's okay because you're a better person because you made the attempt. I don't agree with that at all."

I asked her to give me an example. She said, "I'm a senior, and in the beginning of the year, my goal was to be captain of the soccer team. I didn't get it, and yet you're saying that's okay."

I explained to her that not being selected captain doesn't mean she shouldn't feel disappointed, sad, or even angry. The rest of the conversation went like this:

ED: Did you write your goal down and were you clear and specific?

LAURA: Yes, I was clear and specific. I will be a great captain for my soccer team in my senior year and lead them to a state championship.

ED: Excellent. What were the mini-goals you set for yourself?

LAURA: I brought all my grades up from a C average to a B average, because at my school you can't be captain of any team unless you have a B average or better. I met with every player before the season started to find out what their individual and team goals were. I worked out every day and ate healthy. In my mind, I visualized being captain of the team. I had a positive attitude. I did all of that, and I still didn't achieve my goal.

ED: I know the season is over, but how did your team do?

LAURA: We did okay.

Her friend sitting next to her spoke up and said, "We didn't just do okay, our team made it to the state finals for the first time in school history. We lost, but it was still a great season."

ED: How did you do on an individual basis?

LAURA: I did okay.

Her friend spoke up again and said, "She didn't just do okay. She led the team in assists and was second on the team in scoring."

ED: Are you going to college next year?

LAURA: Yes.

ED: Are you playing soccer there?

LAURA: Yes.

Again, her friend interjected, "She got a scholarship to play."

ED: After looking at all of this, can you really tell me that you're not a better student and soccer player because you made the attempt to be captain? Didn't you help lead your team to a successful season?

LAURA: Looking at it now, I am a better person because I made the attempt, and we did have a winning season. I just never thought of looking at it that way.

Success is a journey, not just a destination!

The world puts so much focus on being No. 1, finishing first, and winning that if you're not careful, you can sell out yourself and others to reach your goal. Social media can be a double-edged sword when it comes to success and self-worth. While it provides a platform for self-expression and connection, it also creates a sense of competition and validation-seeking based on likes, views, and follows. This can lead to a shift in focus from personal growth and fulfillment to external validation and comparison. In essence, you can lose sight of what truly matters to you and what you want to achieve as you become preoccupied with the numbers and metrics that define "social media success." It's important to remember that these metrics do not necessarily equate to real-world success or personal happiness, and your self-worth and purpose should not be defined by them.

Setting goals and deciding where you want to go and what you want to do can, at times, be frustrating. That's especially true if what you're striving for isn't available because you're too young, don't have enough experience, or an unexpected event causes it to be closed or canceled. This was the feeling that an actor shared with me during the COVID-19 pandemic. Brittany had a goal to be an actor on Broadway, but Broadway was closed indefinitely, and she was feeling hopeless. What I said to her was "Yes, Broadway is closed for now, but the big question is: What are you doing right now to prepare yourself for when the doors do open back up and the stage lights come on? Will you be ready?" I challenged her to change her attitude and focus on what she could control right now.

When you're faced with obstacles, it's easy to feel defeated and lose sight of your goals. However, it's important to remember that challenges and setbacks also can be opportunities for growth and progress. As the saying goes, "When one door closes, another one opens." Instead of focusing on what you *can't* do, shift your mindset to what you *can* do to prepare for when the opportunity arises. In Brittany's case, she couldn't perform on Broadway right now, but that didn't mean she couldn't work on improving her craft and preparing for the future. We talked about taking proactive steps, such as taking online acting classes, connecting with others in the industry, and educating herself on the craft of acting.

Success is not just a destination. It's a journey filled with ups and downs, twists and turns, and lessons learned. Don't just focus on the destination, but also appreciate the journey and the person you become along the way. Embrace the challenges as opportunities to grow and learn, for they will shape you into a stronger and more resilient individual. Keep moving forward with purpose and determination, and know that every step you take, no matter how small, brings you closer to the summit of your aspirations. Remember, success is not a one-time event, but a continuous journey of self-improvement and progress.

Just as a sailor may need to change course when the wind shifts, you too may need to adjust your plans and find new ways to reach your destination.

Fordham University in New York has invited me to be the keynote speaker at their New Student Orientation program for the past 22 years. I share strategies with the students to help them make a successful transition into college and give them keys to achieving their goals.

One year, a senior orientation leader came up to me and said, "Hey, you're Ed Gerety. I remember you. You spoke at my orientation when I was a first-year student here."

"Wow, thank you for remembering what I said," I responded.

He said, "Yeah you actually brought me up on-stage and had me do this goal-setting exercise from 'I want' to 'I will.'" I asked if he remembered what his goal was.

He said with a smile, "I will be an Oscar-winning director by the age of 35 here in Manhattan."

"That's awesome!" I responded. "Are you still in film studies here at Fordham?"

He looked at me, laughed, and responded confidently, "No. I started out in film, but then I became more curious and excited about music. The more I learned about the music industry, I realized that was what I wanted to build my career around. So, now I have a new goal."

"What's that?" I asked.

"I will have my own music production company here in Manhattan by the age of 25 representing the top-10 hip-hop artists in the world," he told me.

"That's great! What are you doing now to get closer to that goal?" I asked.

"Right now, I have an internship with Sony in their international marketing department."

"Congratulations!"

Achieving your goals is a journey that requires dedication, perseverance, and resilience. It's not just about following a simple formula or ticking off a checklist of tasks. Along the way, you will encounter obstacles and setbacks, but it's important to remember that these are opportunities for growth and learning. Don't be discouraged by changing course and going in a different direction. Success is not a destination, but a journey of continuous self-improvement and personal growth. Never let the fear of failure or setbacks hinder your progress toward your dreams. Stay focused and keep moving forward, one step at a time. Remember, each stride you make, no matter how small, brings you closer to achieving your goals. Believe in yourself and trust the journey, because with hard work and perseverance, success is within reach.

TURN OBSTACLES INTO OPPORTUNITIES

"Two roads diverged in a wood and I—
I took the one less traveled by,
and that has made all the difference."

—ROBERT FROST

My friend Julia got her first job after college as a sales rep for a pharmaceutical company. They put her through an intensive three-month training program to learn about the company and its products. When the training was complete, she had her first in-person sales call with a doctor who had the largest practice in the area. At the appointment, the person at the front desk escorted her into a small room and said, "The doctor will be with you in a moment."

Twenty minutes later, the doctor walked in, and Julia introduced herself. She was excited to share her information sheet with the doctor and the benefits of the product. However, after she handed him the sheet, the doctor, without saying a word, tore the paper up right in front of her. He then crumpled it into a ball and threw it in the trash as he walked out of the room. Julia was stunned and for a moment thought that maybe this was some practical joke. It was not. As the tears started to well up in her eyes, she walked over to the trash can, picked up the torn and ripped info sheet, put it in her bag, and drove back to her office.

At that moment, there was a part of her that wanted to quit. She felt like a failure and thought that maybe she wasn't cut out for sales. Julia explained to me that this was a defining moment in her career because, instead of giving up, she decided to use the rejection to fuel her fire to keep moving forward.

So what did she do? Back at the office, she carefully taped the info sheet back together piece by piece, rip by rip. Then she had it laminated with a protective plastic layer. Two months later, she set up another appointment with that very same doctor.

This time, when the doctor walked in and recognized her, he stopped and asked, "What are you doing back here, and why do you have that ripped up info sheet all taped up and laminated?"

Julia responded, "This info sheet is the best thing that ever happened to me. Since the last time I was here, I have visited all the other doctors around the area, and the first thing they ask me is 'Why is your info sheet all ripped up and laminated?' And I explain to them, 'Well, the first doctor I saw ripped it up in front of me, didn't say a word, and just threw it in the trash as he walked out. There was no way I was going to let one person take this one possible solution, throw it in the trash, and not even try to see if it can make a difference.'"

The doctor didn't say anything for a few moments. Then he said, "Let's sit down." He apologized by saying, "I'm sorry. That was a bad day, and my behavior was inexcusable. Let me hear about your product."

Julia told me that over the next few years, he became her top client, a good friend, and, in many ways, a mentor. She is now director of sales and marketing for one of the largest pharmaceutical companies in the world.

What if she'd given up when her product was thrown in the trash? What if she'd said, "That's it. I'm done with this job and career path. I quit. I'm out of here."

What if Tom Brady had stopped playing football because he was drafted as the 199th pick in the sixth round of the NFL draft?

~

What if basketball player Michael Jordan had quit after he was cut from his high school basketball team?

What if best-selling author J.K. Rowling gave up on her Harry Potter book after the 12th rejection letter?

You're going to experience people who tell you that you can't achieve your goals, that you're not smart enough or good enough. As Julia's story demonstrates, your defining moments in life don't come from the easy wins and victories. They come when you turn a setback into a great comeback and an obstacle into a new opportunity for growth and success.

PRACTICE THE ART OF SAYING NO

"Daring to set boundaries is about having the courage to love ourselves even when we risk disappointing others."

—BRENÉ BROWN

As I walked off the stage from a live presentation, one of the audience members walked up to me with tears in her eyes and said, "I just feel burnt out. I have so much on my plate. I have no time. I know I can do better. I just don't know what to do or where to start."

As a high achiever, it's often easy to feel this way because you want to say yes to everything. You don't want to miss out on an opportunity. You have a big heart and want to make a difference. On top of that, you don't want to let anyone down. Before you know it, you're going from one meeting to the next, one event to the next, spreading yourself thin, and feeling the same way that person shared with me backstage. The more directions you get pulled in, the less effective you are at each activity you're doing. It's like skimming the surface of the water and never getting the chance to go deeper and explore what more you can learn and discover. When you spread yourself too thin, you can feel like you are not able to give your best to anything.

Staying positive and having a growth mindset is influenced just as much by your ability to say no as it is by being willing to say yes. Saying no takes courage. Saying no means you are saying yes to something bigger. Saying no can be difficult, but it's important to prioritize and focus on what's most important to you and your goals. By saying no, you can avoid feeling overwhelmed and burnt out, and you can give your best to the things that matter most. If the answer is no, you can confidently respond by saying, "Thank you for the invitation and for thinking of me; however, at this time, I'm going to say no. I wish you success."

CELEBRATE THE JOURNEY

"Write your worries in sand, your blessings in stone."
—ELLA WHEELER WILCOX

Achieving your goals without taking the time to acknowledge and celebrate them is like sailing a ship without ever stopping to appreciate the beauty of the ocean. It's like being so focused on reaching the next port that you forget to enjoy the journey and the progress you've made. Just as a sailor takes time to appreciate the stunning sunsets and the calming rhythm of the waves, you also should take a moment to reflect on your accomplishments and savor the feeling of success. By doing so, you can recharge your batteries, gain new perspectives, and set sail toward even greater achievements.

Have you ever gone through a week and not remembered everything you accomplished? Can you remember achieving a goal and just quickly moving on to the next one? One of the mistakes I made early in my career was not taking the time to acknowledge the wins along the way—personally or professionally.

I was so driven and in a rush to keep pushing further and reaching for the next goal that I never took the time to really enjoy the progress I was making. There was no celebration or time for reflecting on what I was learning and how I could improve. It was go, go, go, and then go some more.

As a result, more times than not I felt unsatisfied, tired, and frustrated that things were not perfect. It was challenging to keep a positive attitude and a growth mindset that would give me the confidence to keep moving forward. That all changed when I participated in a coaching program called Strategic Coach©, which helps entrepreneurs reach their full potential. It was there that I was introduced to a new habit called Positive Focus©. This is where you take the time each day, week, month, and year to write down the things you've achieved, the progress you've made, and the great things that have happened to you personally and professionally. You include some thoughts about the people who helped you, why each moment was special, and the next action step to take.

For example, I knew that writing and publishing a book was going to be a big undertaking and take a lot of time and effort. During the process, I took the time to acknowledge the steps that I was accomplishing, whether it was completing the outline of the book, writing the first chapter, or finding an editor. By focusing on the small wins along the way, I was able to feel less stressed and more confident to keep moving forward. I was able to enjoy the journey toward achieving my big goal … which you are now reading.

As I started to do this consistently, I found that my energy began to shift and I became more optimistic about the progress I was making. My mindset became focused on "progress, not perfection." This awareness and appreciation for the small wins, victories, and special moments along the way gives me the confidence and enthusiasm to keep moving forward.

If you're willing to try making positive focus a habit, you'll find that you become more empowered and present to the abundance and love you have in your life. The practice will help you have the strength and courage to be resilient, embrace change, and achieve your goals.

SEIZE THE DAY!

"We are what we repeatedly do.
Excellence, then, is not an act but a habit."

—ARISTOTLE

If you don't take responsibility to create your day, someone will do that for you. When that happens, you give your power away and your priorities get scattered. One of my mentors, Richard O'Donnell, an award-winning educator for more than three decades, taught me the importance of having a daily planner and calendar—one central place to keep track of all my activities, due dates, to-dos, and goals.

I also take time each morning to write in my gratitude journal about the people and things I am grateful for in my life and the progress I'm making. Every day, I write this on the top of my daily planner: "I'm 100% responsible for my life. Seize the day!" I also list my three most important priorities for the day, and I do my positive focus.

These are some of the routines and rituals I do to help me keep a positive attitude and growth mindset. They help me navigate change and unexpected events and empower me to stay calmer and more centered. Every high achiever and peak performer I've ever met or read about has created similar routines that set them up to win each day. Here are a few that people have shared with me.

Kendall is a student-athlete and leader who takes the time each night to line up all her clothes. She charges the electronic devices she will need the following day and checks her alarm clock (twice) to be sure it's set for the right wake-up time. She explained to me that this helps her get a better night's sleep because she has the peace of mind of knowing that she is ready for tomorrow.

Terri, a successful entrepreneur, has a bowl of oatmeal and blueberries every morning. She said, "I know that when I have breakfast, it increases my energy levels and improves my concentration."

Others have shared with me that they make their bed, pray, meditate, exercise, read, write, play their guitar, or spend time in nature. Like anything, though, consistency is key! If you only do these things once in a while, then once in a while you feel happy about where you are and where you're going.

Setting your day up for success will give you clarity, and with that clarity, you will get more confidence. The more confidence you have, the more unstoppable you feel to truly seize the day!

MOVING FORWARD
REFLECTION & ACTION

*"If you don't choose your greatness,
someone else will choose your mediocrity."*

—ED GERETY

YOU CAN ONLY REACH GOALS YOU SET. WHAT DO YOU WANT TO ACHIEVE?

dream: a cherished aspiration, ambition, or ideal

goal: the object of a person's ambition or effort; an aim or desired result

1. What are you curious about?

2. Growing up, what was one of your dreams?

3. Who is someone you know who has made their dream come true?

4. What is one of the first steps in turning your dreams into an achievable goal?

5. Share a goal that you achieved and what you had to overcome to make it happen.

6. What are three big goals you are committed to accomplishing?

7. What are three skills or strengths that will help you reach your goals?

8. Apply the goal-setting formula in this chapter to one of your goals.

9. What will you do if you don't reach your goal?

10. Create a dream board.

DREAM BOARD ACTIVITY

What is a dream board?

A dream board is a powerful visual representation of your goals and dreams. It's a poster you create that contains both pictures and words that describe your goals and dreams. It represents who you are, where you want to go, and what you are committed to achieving. It's not just a collage of pretty pictures—it's a powerful tool that has been used by thousands of individuals to help make their dreams come true. Dream boards are also referred to as vision boards, goal maps, roadmaps, and treasure maps.

Materials:
~ 7–10 magazines that can be cut up
~ A picture of yourself
~ Poster board
~ Scissors
~ Markers
~ Glue stick

How does it work?
What you think about, you become. What you focus on in your life, you attract. Creating a dream board plays an important role in achieving your goals and living your dreams. Once you complete your dream board, you should place it somewhere that is highly visible to you on a daily basis, such as your bedroom, office space, or living room. Take a few minutes every day to look at your dream board and reflect on what you are committed to achieving, experiencing, or being.

How do I assemble my dream board?

Find a peaceful workspace that will allow you to concentrate and think deeply about yourself and your dreams and goals. To start, take the poster board and glue the picture of yourself in the middle of it. Next, go through the magazines to find pictures and words that symbolize and describe your goals and dreams. You want to find images and words that describe who you are, where you want to go, and what you are committed to achieving. You also can draw and write on the board if you can't find what you're looking for.

The organization of this board is entirely up to you! You can organize it by category (relationships, career, school) or you can dedicate the whole board to achieving one big goal (divided into mini-goals). This is a tool that is supposed to help you, so you should set it up however it makes sense to you.

Once you decide on the layout of your board, glue the words and images to the board and make sure they are secure. Once your board is complete, you can use it as a daily reference to remind yourself of your goals and help you stay on track. Make a conscious effort every day to look at the board. It should be the first thing you look at when you wake up and the last thing you look at before you go to bed. You can even take a picture of it and make it the screensaver on your computer or phone.

Anchored in Accountability

*"We must all face the choice between
what is right and what is easy."*

—ALBUS DUMBLEDORE, HARRY POTTER

THE POWER OF CHOICE

*"Everything can be taken from a man but one thing:
the last of the human freedoms—to choose one's attitude
in any given set of circumstances, to choose one's own way."*

—VIKTOR FRANKL

Viktor Frankl, a Holocaust survivor and psychiatrist, believed that although we may not be able to control the circumstances we face, we always have a choice in how we respond to them. During World War II, Frankl was interned in four different concentration camps, but he survived. In his book *Man's Search for Meaning*, he described his experiences and what he derived from the ordeal. Frankl wrote: "Everything can be taken from a man but one thing: the last of the human freedoms—to choose one's attitude in any given set of circumstances, to choose one's own way."

Frankl believed that even in the most extreme situations, such as the concentration camps he endured, individuals could choose their own way of responding to their circumstances. He observed that some people were able to find meaning and purpose in their suffering, while others succumbed to despair.

His message was one of hope and resilience, emphasizing that even in the most challenging circumstances, you can still exercise your freedom to choose your own attitude and response. He believed that by finding meaning and purpose in your life, you can transcend your circumstances and find a sense of inner peace and fulfillment.

A student named Alex was faced with a tough decision: Should she study for her upcoming exam or go out with friends? Alex knew that studying would bring her closer to her goal of getting good grades and eventually getting into a good college. On the other hand, going out with friends may give her short-term happiness, but it may also lead to a lower grade on the exam. Alex knew that she had the power to choose, and the consequences would either bring her closer to her goals or push them further away. She took responsibility for her decision and chose to study for the exam. As a result, Alex got a good grade on her exam and felt proud of her choice. Your academic decisions are only one area of your life where you have the power to choose.

You already know that your attitude, goals, and giving your best effort are all choices. Your choices are also responsible for how you resolve a conflict, the relationships you have, and what you do socially.

Sometimes the consequences last not only a month or a year, but forever. I will never forget the student who came up to me after one of my presentations.

"Mr. Gerety, I wish that my boyfriend had been in your program today."

I looked at her and asked, "Where is your boyfriend? Is he sick? Does he go to another school?"

She said, "No, he's dead. He died last fall."

I said, "I'm sorry," then I asked, "How did he die?"

She said, "Well, you see, there was this big party. You know the kind of party everybody knows about, that everybody talks about?"

I said, "Yeah."

She said, "Well, this was *that* kind of party, but it was okay."

"What do you mean it was okay?"

"Well, everybody was being responsible. See, nobody was drinking and driving. Everybody made the deal. They would just show up at this house and they'd spend the night. Even a couple parents knew about it.

"Well, I didn't drink, and around 11:30 that night, I said goodbye to my boyfriend and my friends and walked home. I was told that my boyfriend and his friends stayed up that night. They played drinking games, and they did toasts and cheers. Around 2:30 that morning, my boyfriend became very sick. But, being the good friends they were, they stayed with him as he got sick, and when he was done, they cleaned him up. They gave him a fresh T-shirt, and they gave him the biggest bed in the house to let him sleep it off—laughing as they shut the door about how drunk their good friend had gotten."

She looked at me and she said, "Mr. Gerety, he never woke up, because he died of alcohol poisoning." She asked, "Could you do me a favor? Could you please share this story wherever you speak? So that maybe somebody else's boyfriend, friend, classmate, or teammate won't have what happened to him happen to them?"

As John Alston said, "We have the freedom to choose, but we do not have the freedom of consequence." What choices are you making in your life right now? What are you texting, posting, and sharing on social media? Those are all choices: Delete does not mean that it's gone. It just means you can no longer see it. In the world you live in today, it's not just how you represent yourself to your friends and peers, it's how you represent yourself to the entire world through your social media channels.

One person shared with me how this one decision kept her from getting her dream job as a pilot at a major airline. She had all the credentials, scored at the top of her class, and had an amazing interview. Unfortunately, when the airline checked her social media channels, they found things that were inappropriate and not in alignment with the mission of the company. Today, you can make the choice to reset, to step up, and to create new habits that will lead you toward creating and living a life you love.

Here are five steps to making a positive choice:

1. **Identify the decision:** Clearly define the decision that needs to be made and determine why it's important.

2. **Gather information:** Collect as much relevant information as possible, including pros and cons, risks and benefits, and potential outcomes.

3. **Consider alternatives:** Explore different options and alternatives and evaluate their potential impact and feasibility. Write them down.

4. **Evaluate the options:** Weigh the advantages and disadvantages of each option, taking into account your goals, values, and priorities.

5. **Make a decision:** Once you've evaluated the options, make a decision that aligns with your goals, values, and priorities.

It's important to remember that making a positive choice is not about choosing the "right" option, it's about making a decision that is the right fit for the way you live your life. By following these steps, you can make a decision that is informed, thoughtful, and in line with your personal goals and values.

DIVE BENEATH THE SURFACE

"We don't need to share the same opinions as others, but we need to be respectful."

—TAYLOR SWIFT

I was having lunch with a group of students in their school cafeteria, when, at the table across from us, I heard four students laughing loudly. One of them said, "Look at him over there you guys. Look at him!"

At the other end of their table, sitting by himself, was a student eating his lunch. The first student went on to exclaim, "He has the same shirt on that he's been wearing all week! Can you believe it? That is so disgusting." Another chimed in, "Yeah, he's in one of my classes. He's such a joke."

I looked over to see if the young man could hear what they were saying about him. I knew that he could because he was hunched over his sandwich, which he was now quickly trying to finish.

As a bystander, I had a responsibility to stop the teasing, to get help to stop it, or to remove him from the situation. I also knew something about that young man that they didn't know, something the principal of that school had shared with me earlier that morning. So I got up and walked over to confront the four students. Were they sixth-graders or fourth-graders? Neither. All four of them were seniors in high school.

I politely said, "Excuse me, can I please speak to all of you out in the hallway?"

One of the young ladies looked at me and asked sarcastically, "Who are you?"

Showing them my visitor pass, I said, "My name is Ed Gerety. I'm a guest speaker today at your school. Can I please speak to the four of you out in the hallway for a moment?" They reluctantly got up, mumbling about how ridiculous it was to have their lunch interrupted, especially as seniors.

Out in the hallway, I asked them, "Do you know why the student you were making fun of probably has been wearing the same shirt for the past week?"

One of the students stepped forward to get right in my face and answered mockingly, "I don't know, because he's a loser? What's the big deal?"

I shared with them how after school, before all the cars and buses arrive, his mother picks him up and they drive an hour and a half to the children's hospital to see his little brother who is sick. He spends the night next to his little brother because he's scared, they're best friends, and he's the only brother he has. He gets up at 5:30 in the morning and drives back to school with his mom.

"Did you know that?" I asked them.

The students tried to defend themselves by simply saying, "Well, we didn't know."

My only response to them was, "How were you supposed to know?" They then quietly walked back into the cafeteria to finish their lunch. The student they were laughing at had already gone.

You don't know everyone's story! You should never judge a book by its cover, and yet that is exactly what we often do as human beings. We judge, ridicule, and make fun of others to get a cheap laugh from our friends or to make us feel better about ourselves. It's up to you and me to make the conscious choice to not participate in conversations that hurt others. Our words and our actions will always do one of two things: tear people down or build people up.

Often, people will come up to me after one of my programs and say, "Can I ask you a question?" The majority of the time it's not a question. It's their story that they want to share. They don't want advice or answers. They simply want to be heard and understood.

Luke was one of those individuals who shared his story with me. "My mom is a raging alcoholic, and some nights I have to break up fistfights between her and one of my other siblings. I go to bed in tears some nights not knowing what to do."

Another person, Courtney, told me how one morning she came to school just after she saw her dad being taken away in an ambulance. "As I was walking to my locker, while my mind was racing with thoughts on what is going on with my dad, one of my friends came up to me. Apparently, I did something to make her mad at me, and she said, 'No one cares about you anyway. You're just a nobody.' It's never right to say that to anyone, but she had no idea what happened two hours before I came to school."

Luke's and Courtney's stories are a powerful reminder that you never truly know what someone else is going through. You may see them at school, work, or in your daily life, but you don't always know what battles they are fighting behind closed doors.

Luke's struggles with his mother's alcoholism and the violent fights in his home are unimaginable to many of us. Yet he remains resilient, recognizing that he is not alone in his struggles and finding strength in the shared experiences of others. Luke's story shows that you should approach each person with compassion and kindness, for you never know the weight they are carrying.

Similarly, Courtney's experience demonstrates the importance of not judging others, especially when you have no idea what they are going through. Her friend's hurtful words only added to her already difficult situation, and it was only through her own pain that she realized the impact our words and actions can have on others.

Both of these stories are a testament to the resilience and strength of the human spirit, even in the face of immense challenges. They remind us to be mindful of the struggles of those around us and always to approach others with empathy and understanding, for you never know what challenges they are facing.

WAVES OF RESPECT

"Do things for people not because of who they are or what they do in return, but because of who you are."

—HAROLD S. KUSHNER

Are you supposed to be respectful to others just because they might have something going on in their life that you don't know about or because they may have been through something incredibly challenging? Yes! Of course. However, you and I should have that respect and compassion for one another "just because." Just because we are all unique and special. We must celebrate what makes us different and embrace what we have in common. That's how we grow and work together to build a strong community, a positive workplace, and meaningful connections. It's when you live and lead your life with this grace and civility that you can create and live a life that you love.

Sometimes you might think that it's okay to tease others if they are your close friends or teammates. One of the most important aspects of friendship is mutual respect and support. While it may seem harmless to engage in playful teasing with close friends, it's important to remember that words have the power to hurt. Even if the intention is not to harm, the impact can still be painful.

Think about Sophie, the basketball player, who shared with me how she was laughed at by her teammates and close friends. While they may have thought they were just joking around, their words caused her to feel isolated and hurt. She deserved better from her friends, who should have been building her up instead of tearing her down. Your friends should never talk behind your back, they should have your back!

Here are some powerful words of encouragement to help boost someone's spirits:

1. "You've got this! I believe in you and your abilities."

2. "I am so proud of you and all that you've accomplished. Keep up the great work!"

3. "I know things might seem tough right now, but remember that you are strong and capable of overcoming any obstacle."

4. "Don't give up! I'm here for you and we'll get through this together."

5. "You inspire me with your dedication and perseverance. Keep pushing forward and great things will come your way."

So let's make a commitment to lift each other up, even in moments of lighthearted teasing. Let's choose to use our words to encourage and support one another, not to bring each other down. Let's be the kind of friends who build each other up and create a safe and supportive environment in which we can all thrive.

TOGETHER WE RISE

*"For there is always light,
if only we're brave enough to see it.
If only we're brave enough to be it."*

—AMANDA GORMAN

During one of my presentations, I invited 20 people on-stage. They were given instructions to walk around the stage and not make eye contact with anyone they passed. Instantly, almost all of them changed their posture and put their heads down. The exercise continued for another minute, and I asked the audience to share what they observed. One person commented that as the participants looked down, their shoulders hunched over, and their pace was slow and lethargic. They looked like they were shuffling their feet rather than walking. Another person shared that there was no energy, no connection, and that they looked sad. Another person pointed out that they looked like they were lost and didn't belong.

Their observations were a reminder that there are people in their community who feel invisible, left out, and turned away. There are people whose good intentions to be kind are often mocked or simply ignored.

This part of the exercise was a great visual of what can happen in their school, company, or organization if they don't make the choice to look up and truly connect with others, to acknowledge them and let them know that they matter.

The volunteers onstage were then asked to repeat the exercise, except this time they were to make eye contact for two to three seconds with each person they passed. Instantly, almost all of them changed their body language and put their heads up. It quickly became apparent that the eye contact caused each person to smile and, in some cases, laugh. The group that had seemed so distant from each other now seemed to be more connected and united. They were no longer scattered all over the stage, but had formed a small huddle at the center of it. As one person commented, "You can see there is a sense of acceptance, belonging, and respect among one another."

Want to make someone feel valued and appreciated? Try these five strategies:

1. **Listen actively:** When someone is speaking to you, give them your full attention. Listen actively by making eye contact, nodding your head, and asking open-ended questions to show that you are engaged and interested in what they have to say.

2. **Validate their feelings:** Acknowledge the other person's emotions and feelings by using statements such as "I understand how you feel," "I'm sorry you're going through this," or "That must be really tough for you." This lets them know that their feelings are valid and that you are there to support them.

3. **Avoid judging or criticizing:** When someone shares something with you, it's important not to judge or criticize them. Instead, try to understand their perspective and show empathy toward their situation.

4. **Show appreciation:** Let the person know that you value and appreciate them by expressing gratitude

for their presence in your life. This can be as simple as saying "Thank you for being there for me" or "I'm grateful to have you in my life."

5. **Create a safe space:** Make the other person feel safe and comfortable by creating an environment where they feel free to express themselves without fear of judgment. Be open, nonjudgmental, and compassionate toward their thoughts and feelings. This will help them feel seen, heard, and accepted for who they are.

STAND TALL

"With great power comes great responsibility."
—UNCLE BEN, SPIDER-MAN

As a leader, one of the most impactful choices you can make is to lead by example. Your personal responsibility to practice compassion and respect becomes even more crucial when you are in a leadership position.

From a young age, I was taught that the greatest influence a leader can have is to lead by example. As Ralph Waldo Emerson famously said, "Your actions speak so loudly that I cannot hear what you are saying." However, it wasn't until a particular experience I had that I fully understood the power of this lesson.

During my senior year of high school, I had the honor of serving as one of the captains of our school's football team. As the season began, a new player named John joined our team. Though he was not as experienced or naturally talented as the other players, he had a positive attitude and was doing his best to learn the game. However, I soon noticed that some of my teammates were not treating John fairly during practice. They were taking advantage of his small size by tackling him harder and pushing him to the ground.

As a captain, I knew I had to take action. I gathered a few players and spoke up for John. I reminded them that he was doing his best and deserved the same respect as any other teammate. Unfortunately, my request was ignored, and they accused me of being too soft. Regrettably, I backed down and did not pursue it any further. However, my decision to remain silent had consequences.

Four games later, our coach delivered the sad news that John had quit the team. The season went on and we eventually made it to the state championship game. During that game the other team called a timeout with only 30 seconds left in the game. We were about to win our school's first state championship title. I went to the sidelines to celebrate with my family and friends. Who was also standing there? John. He looked at me, smiled and gave me a quick congratulatory nod.

A couple of weeks later, my mom saw his mom in the grocery store. John's mom told her, "I wish that my son had stuck the season out. He so loves football, and he enjoyed going to practice and learning how to play. His younger brothers also thought it was so cool that he was on the team." Although I wasn't directly involved in treating John unfairly on the football field, I unintentionally deprived him of that experience. Instead of remaining passive, I could have taken proactive steps such as informing my fellow captains about the situation, initiating conversations with the coaches, and providing more support and encouragement to John. This experience taught me a valuable lesson about being a leader. Just as a lighthouse beacon shines its light equally for all ships at sea to guide them to safety in dangerous waters, true leaders have the power to make *everyone* feel included and valued. But it takes more than just saying the right things. Leaders must take action and stand up for what's right, even when it's unpopular, just like a ship's captain who steers the vessel through rough currents and storms. Let your light shine bright and guide the way for others, while being a beacon of hope that inspires and motivates them to follow their own path.

MOVING FORWARD
REFLECTION & ACTION

*"When you let go of the need to control
and simply trust in the unfolding of life,
you open yourself to infinite possibilities."*

—MICHAEL A. SINGER

YOU ARE 100% RESPONSIBLE
FOR YOUR LIFE.
WHAT CHOICES ARE YOU MAKING?

respect: esteem for or a sense of the worth or excellence of a person, a personal quality or ability, or something considered as a manifestation of a personal quality or ability

responsibility: the state or fact of being responsible, answerable, or accountable for something within one's power, control, or management

1. Can you recall a time when you witnessed someone being irresponsible? How did this situation make you feel?

2. Have you ever had to take responsibility for a mistake you made? Can you share the experience and what you learned from it?

3. What are some common habits or traits of responsible individuals, and how can you work on cultivating these traits in yourself?

4. Have you ever made a judgment about a person or situation without having all the information? How did this make you feel?

5. Can you name three friends who respect your choices, and what qualities do they have that make them respectful?

6. Why is it essential to take a step back before reacting to a person or situation?

7. What are three actions you could take to show respect for others?

8. What are three things you could do to show respect for yourself?

9. Can you share an inspirational quote about respect or compassion that resonates with you?

10. In what ways do responsibility and respect intersect, and how can practicing both benefit individuals and society?

4

A Guiding Light

*"Let us fill our hearts with our own compassion—
towards ourselves and towards all living beings."*

—THICH NHAT HANH

BE A GOOD PERSON

*"Spread love everywhere you go.
Let no one ever come to you without leaving happier."*
—MOTHER TERESA

Sometimes, in the midst of our fast-paced and hectic routines, an unexpected act of kindness can make all the difference. One day my wife, Suzanne, and I were going through a Dunkin' Donuts drive-through and she was having a hard time placing the order. Our two kids, ages 5 and 7, were in the back seat, crying. These were not just little cries, either. It was like *Jurassic Park's* raptor one and raptor two. They were almost deafening. We drove up to the window to pay, and the cashier appeared to be laughing at us.

"What's so funny?" my wife asked.

The cashier replied with a big smile, "The car in front of you just paid for your bagels, juice, and coffee. They could hear your kids crying and told me to tell you to enjoy the little ones, because they grow up so fast."

Suzanne and I started laughing and said thank you. As we drove away, my wife said, "Woo-hoo, let them scream!" An act of kindness from a stranger turned a stressful moment into one that was light and fun.

That's what being kind to others does. It changes people's emotions and helps put life's stressful moments into perspective.

~

Every day presents an opportunity to practice the art of kindness. Like an artist with a canvas, you have infinite ways to express and share kindness. This beautiful art form has the power to touch, move, and inspire people in ways that are beyond measure.

Kindness reminds us that we are all interconnected as human beings and that there is good in the world. It can be as simple as a warm smile, a friendly greeting, or a small act of courtesy, yet it has the potential to open someone's heart and change their life forever.

Although there may be those who don't respond in kind, never let that stop you from reaching out to the next person. For every negative encounter, there are countless more opportunities to create a positive impact. Let us continue to spread kindness and make the world a better place, one act at a time.

The journey of life is full of surprises, and sometimes, even the most unexpected encounters can lead to important life lessons. My son, Ryan, was attending a lacrosse camp at Harvard University in Cambridge, Mass. It was our first time visiting the famous university. Exploring the campus and its historic structures, we came across Harvard Stadium and decided to go in. As we walked around, we saw a student-athlete sitting in the bleachers wearing a Harvard Soccer jacket. I asked him, "Excuse me, Do you play soccer here?"

He replied, "Yes, I do. I'm currently a junior here."

"That's awesome," I said as I introduced myself and

Ryan to him. I explained why we were there and shared that Ryan, who was entering his first year of high school, had a goal of playing lacrosse in college. "If you don't mind me asking, what is one of the most important things you learned on your journey in becoming a student-athlete in college?"

~

He looked at me and then at Ryan, and said, "You know what? At a certain point, everyone who applies here has a high GPA and SAT score and excels at a particular extracurricular activity. So I think the most important thing to do, if you want to go to Harvard or any other great college, is to be a good person."

I looked at Ryan with a big smile on my face, because this was something that I had told him and his sister since they were little: Be a good person. To have Ryan hear it from a student-athlete at Harvard made it that much more special and significant. Integrity, courage, and compassion are the key qualities of a "good person." They are the anchors that keep a person steady amidst the stormy seas of life. They will help you navigate through challenges and opportunities alike, so you can ultimately arrive at the shores of a fulfilling life.

HAVE A KIND HEART

"Nothing is impossible; the word itself says 'I'm possible'!"
—AUDREY HEPBURN

The power of kindness and generosity can have a remarkable impact on the world around you. It can transform individuals, communities, and even entire nations. Jim Johnson is one of those individuals who has chosen to live his life with this philosophy at the forefront of everything he does. As an award-winning coach, author, and teacher, Coach Johnson has spent more than 30 years developing winning high school basketball teams. But his greatest achievement, as he shared with me on my podcast, *Parents Navigating the Teen Years*, is not the 428 career victories he's had as a coach. Instead, it's the profound impact he's had on his players' lives, helping them win at the game of life.

One of those players was an autistic boy named Jason McElwain, nicknamed J-Mac. During one of the final games of the season, Coach Johnson put J-Mac, who was the team manager at the time, into the game. He scored 20 points in just over four minutes, including six 3-point baskets. This kindhearted gesture from the coach and courageous performance by J-Mac was featured in major news outlets across the country. It inspired so many people because it showed the power of the human spirit—that anything is possible if you believe and have others who believe in you.

Coach Johnson's philosophy on leadership and life is one that shines a spotlight on others and gives everyone the chance to make their dreams come true. Unfortunately, not everyone shares this belief. There are those who see the world through a lens of scarcity and negativity, always looking for what's wrong instead of what's right. For them, the world is a place where someone is always out to take advantage, steal, or deceive. In this way of thinking, there's no room for kindness, generosity, or abundance. Winning in life is not a possibility, and merely surviving becomes the only option. Despite this, Coach Johnson's dedication to his philosophy and his ability to inspire others to adopt it has proven that there is another way to approach life, one that leads to a more gratifying and fulfilling way of living.

LISTEN TO YOUR HEART

"All I can tell you really is if you get to the point where someone is telling you that you are not great or not good enough, just follow your heart and don't let anybody crush your dream."

—PATTI LABELLE

In a world where stress and anxiety are prevalent, people are constantly searching for ways to improve their health and well-being. For some, traditional methods like medication or therapy may not be effective, leading them to explore alternative options. This is where my friend Daryl Browne and his wife, Nastia, come in. As co-owners of Soleil's Salt Cave in Exeter, N.H., they have created a unique space for people to relax, unwind, and improve their health using the power of salt therapy. The cave, encased in 22,000 pounds of the world's oldest salt—Himalayan salt—has two chambers that offer visitors a chance to experience the benefits of breathing salt-infused air. As a frequent visitor to the cave, I can personally attest to the transformative effects of this natural therapy.

But what inspired Daryl and Nastia to create this unique space? Their daughter Soleil's battle with infant eczema sparked their mission to create an environment that promotes healing, wellness, and connection. As the Soleil community continues to grow and their business thrives, I asked Daryl how he has managed the challenges of building and maintaining a successful business. He shared that every decision he makes is grounded in his guiding philosophy of staying true to their values and staying connected to what really matters.

In a world that often values profits over purpose, it's easy to get swept up in external pressures and forget to listen to your own heart. To help find clarity and direction, Daryl offered three questions to ask yourself when making important decisions:

+ Is this opportunity congruent with my values, goals, and what truly matters to me?

+ Have I sought out trusted individuals to discuss this decision with?

+ Have I taken the time to reflect and be quiet with my own thoughts and listen to my heart?

As you navigate the complexities of life, these questions can serve as a compass, guiding you toward a heart-driven approach to creating a fulfilling and purposeful life.

The first time I took my daughter, Shannon, on an airplane, she heard the following instructions from the flight attendant: "In the event of an emergency, please put on your own oxygen mask before assisting others."

She asked me, "Why would you do that dad? Shouldn't you help others first?"

I explained to her that you put your oxygen mask on first because if you run out of oxygen, you can't help anyone else. Those instructions are important to follow, not just when you are on an airplane, but in your everyday life. You can only give to others what you give to yourself first.

There was a time in my life when I had forgotten that life lesson. I was juggling the responsibilities of being a dad and a husband with those of running my own business. There was always a friend to meet and an event to attend. These were all wonderful gifts, but I started to feel burnt out, overwhelmed, and tired. In all of the going, doing, and "busyness," I was living on autopilot, completely inattentive to my own well-being. I neglected my physical, mental, and spiritual health, refusing to make time for the things that truly mattered, such as exercise, reading, journaling, prayer, and quiet reflection. I failed to prioritize my own needs and completely lost touch with how I was truly feeling. After much contemplation,

I came to a powerful realization: Those activities and routines that I once considered to be mere indulgences or reserved for when I have free time were, in fact, essential for my well-being. They were not merely "wants," but "needs" that would provide me with the vigor, endurance, and drive necessary to cherish the people I hold dear and cherish the defining moments in my life. They were, in fact, a lighthouse beaming with clarity and guidance for my journey ahead. No longer were they mere indulgences or distractions; instead, they were the fuel that would power me through any storm. I recognized that to truly love and cherish those I hold dear, I must first honor and cherish myself. As the tides may change, always remember that genuine kindness toward others stems from first being kind to yourself.

UNITED WE STAND

"You are not a drop in the ocean.
You are the entire ocean in a drop."

—RUMI

The choices you make today can have a profound impact on your future and the lives of those around you. Each decision you make creates a ripple effect that can extend far beyond your immediate circumstances, shaping the trajectory of your life and influencing the lives of others in ways you may never fully comprehend. Whether you call it karma, the law of cause and effect, or simply the power of your actions, there is no denying that what you send out comes back to you in some form or another. It's the belief that negative actions can pull and push you and others backward while your positive actions can propel you forward and infuse you and your team with confidence.

I experienced this firsthand during my senior year of high school when I was playing football. Our team had not had a winning season in several years, with records of 1-7, 2-6, and 4-4. There was a climate of big egos and selfishness. We had excellent coaches and talent, but the lack of trust and accountability among the players stopped any real teamwork or success. We knew we had to change the culture on and off the field if we were going to have a winning season.

One example of doing that was changing the tradition of one of the most dreaded practices for the underclassmen: the "senior crawl." Once a season, after practice, all players except seniors had to lie on their stomachs in full equipment in a horizontal line. When the whistle blew, they had to crawl 50 yards through dust and dirt. As they were doing this, the seniors would walk around, grab their legs, and pull them back to the starting line, making the crawl an exhausting and humiliating experience for players continually being pulled back.

When it came time for this ritual to happen in our senior year, we decided that instead of pulling players back, we would pull everyone forward. As we did this, we told the players that this was the new tradition and that the only way we would win this year is if we had one another's backs. "United We Stand. Divided We Fall" became our motto. This was a defining moment in the season when we learned from past mistakes and put the team above any individual or tradition. We went on to achieve a 10-0 record and won the first and only state football championship in school history. That championship team had every class grade represented in the starting lineup. United we stood!

As hard as we try to be kind to others, sometimes they will not respond in the same way. I can remember wishing a person a great day, only to have them respond back sarcastically, "What's so great about it?" Ouch! Don't let the small percentage of people who do this discourage you from reaching out to the next person.

A small act of kindness, even just a kind word, can have a significant impact on someone's life. I was reminded of this when my wife, Suzanne, received an email from Kerry, a fellow parent. In it Kerry shared how, a year earlier, we were all at a swim meet together watching our daughters swim. As we watched, Suzanne complimented Kerry on her daughter's performance, saying "Wow. She's doing great." That small act of recognition meant so much to Kerry because, in 12 years of being involved in that swim club, no one had ever acknowledged her daughter's success. It encouraged Kerry to stick with her child's sports commitment, even on challenging days.

In the email she expressed her gratitude to Suzanne for that moment and let us know that her daughter is now swimming competitively in college. A kind word can go a long way, and you never know how it might impact someone's life.

Your actions can have a ripple effect that extends far beyond your immediate circumstances, and that was certainly the case for our football team. By changing the culture and putting the team first, we were able to achieve something that had never been done before in our school's history. It was a powerful lesson that we carried with us long after the season was over. But as much as you might try to be kind to others, you can't always control how they respond to you. There will always be people who are negative or dismissive. Don't let that keep you from making a connection with the next person. As my wife's experience showed, even a small act of kindness can have a significant impact on someone's life. It's a reminder that you should always strive to lift others up, even in the face of adversity or negativity.

MOVING FORWARD
REFLECTION & ACTION

"The most noble thing you can do
is be kind, generous, and loving to yourself and others."

—ED GERETY

KINDNESS ALWAYS COUNTS: HOW CAN YOU CREATE A RIPPLE EFFECT?

kindness: the quality of being friendly, generous, and considerate

generosity: the quality of being kind and generous

1.   What are five things that make you smile?

2.   Give examples of how you can practice self-care
     and be kind to yourself.

3.   What are some ways that acts of kindness can
     impact the community or society as a whole? How
     can small acts of kindness create a ripple effect?

4.   How can individuals cultivate kindness and
     compassion towards others in their daily lives? What
     are some activities or hobbies that bring you joy?
     How do they contribute to your overall well-being?

5.   Can you share a specific example of a challenge or
     obstacle you overcame in your life? What did you
     learn from the experience, and how did it shape you
     as a person?

6.   Why is it important to appreciate your own qualities
     and strengths? How can this practice help you build
     confidence and self-esteem?

7.   In what ways does showing kindness to others
     benefit both the recipient and the giver? Can you
     think of any examples where you experienced this
     firsthand?

8.   How can having a positive role model or mentor
     impact a person's life? Can you discuss the qualities
     that you admire in your role model and how they have
     influenced you?

9. What are some common things that make people happy or bring them joy? Are these experiences universal, or do they vary from person to person?

10. Can you recall a situation where repeating positive self-talk strengthened your self-confidence and empowered you to pursue your goals?

Examples of acts of kindness that you can do every day:

~ Smile at a friend, co-worker, or stranger

~ Offer a simple wave

~ Open or hold the door for someone

~ Say please and thank you

~ Cook for your family

~ Tell friends that you appreciate them

~ Send someone a handwritten thank-you note

~ Ask people how they are and how their day was

~ Really listen when people speak with you

~ Put away the dishes or laundry

~ Give a genuine compliment

~ Shop or run an errand for people who can't do it for themselves

~ Make eye contact

5

The Rising Tide
That Lifts All Ships

*"Gratitude unlocks the fullness of life.
It turns what we have into enough, and more.
It turns denial into acceptance, chaos into order,
confusion into clarity. It can turn a meal into a feast,
a house into a home, a stranger into a friend."*

—MELODY BEATTIE

WAVES OF GRATITUDE

"Enjoy the little things in life, for one day you'll look back and realize they were big things."

—KURT VONNEGUT

As you navigate through life's waters, it's easy to become so focused on going in the right direction that you forget to enjoy the beauty of the little things around you. Brett was a 13-year-old who was blind, and he came up to me after a presentation and asked if he could get an idea of what I looked like. I said yes, rather tentatively, as I was not sure how he was going to do that.

He took his hand and put it on top of my head, smiled, and said, "You are about this tall." We both laughed as Brett went on to describe how he imagined my appearance to be.

In talking with Brett, I could see that he had a great sense of appreciation for the abilities that he *did* have. His attitude of gratitude was going to help him persevere, be resilient, and achieve his goals.

After hearing this story, Jessica approached me, introduced herself, and shared that she also was blind and could relate to Brett's positive outlook on life. She said, "I'm thankful for the senses I still have, and I try to bring humor to situations that might be uncomfortable. I love roller coasters and have been on ones all over, from Walt Disney World and Six Flags to Hershey Park in Pennsylvania. A Lot of my friends are afraid of roller coasters because of how high and fast they are. But I'm not afraid."

"Why?" I asked.

She smiled, laughed, and replied, "Because I can't see them!"

We often get so caught up in the busyness of our lives that we can forget to appreciate the simple things that make life special. You take your health, relationships, and even your freedom for granted. You assume you'll always have what you have. As a result, the gifts you have in life often only become present to you when you lose them.

Christina, a basketball player, experienced this when she couldn't play for 10 months because of a knee injury that required surgery. She said, "That gave me a whole new appreciation for the game I love and my ability to play it." It could be a season-ending injury, a missed opportunity, or an illness that reminds us to be thankful. However, the most significant time that you realize this is when someone you love dies. It's in those moments that you are truly reminded of what is most important in life. You take the time to reflect and even say to yourself, "I wish … I wish I could just call that person one more time, write that person one more letter, tell that person the three most important words of all: 'I love you.'"

As you grow older and develop as a leader, you need to say "I love you" and "I care about you" not less often, but more often.

In my live speaking presentations, when I talk with audiences about being grateful, I go around the room and ask individuals this question: "If you could call someone right now and let them know how much you appreciate them, whom would you call?" The answers are consistent: "my mom," "my dad," "my grandma," "my sister." Eventually, I bring one of those individuals onstage and have them call that person in front of the entire audience.

On one occasion, I brought up a young man who said he would call his mom. As he took out his phone, he asked me, "Dude, for real? You want me to call her right now?" I told him yes.

When his mom answered, he said, "Hey, Mom, it's Alex, your son. No, Mom, I'm not in trouble. Mom, listen, I'm just calling you to tell you that I love you."

I could hear his mom exclaim, "What?"

"I'm just calling to tell you that I love you, mom."

The mom took a deep breath and said, "I love you too, Alex. Now, let me speak to the principal."

When I did this exercise during a high school assembly, a senior said he would call his sister. When I asked him to call her, he turned a pale white and replied, "We don't have to."

"What do you mean?" I asked.

He pointed up to what appeared to be the sky and said, "She's up there."

My heart dropped. After what seemed to be the longest pause, he continued, "She's up there ... in the bleachers."

I gasped in relief and said, "Let's go tell her."

We walked up to the ninth-grade section of the bleachers. The sister was as red as a tomato, and all her friends had their heads down in embarrassment, except for one who was taking a selfie. As all 1,500 students watched, he looked at his sister and said, "Hey, sis, I know we've been through a lot together, but I will always be there for you, and I love you."

There's likely no one in your life asking you to make those calls while onstage in front of hundreds of people, but it's still important to make them. As one person shared with me, "When I made that phone call and said 'I love you' to my mom, my walls came crashing down and the amount of emotion I felt was overwhelming. Everything coursed through me, from how nervous I was to how much I loved my family to every emotion I have ever felt."

Dean, another student, shared with me that he didn't make a phone call but did take the time to write a letter. "Writing a letter home to a loved one allowed me to tell my dying grandfather things I otherwise wouldn't have said before he passed. The things I said meant a lot to him and my family, and some of my letter was read aloud at his funeral service. I wanted to thank you for that experience. You inspired me to tell him how I felt before it was too late."

There are many ways to express your gratitude and appreciation to another person. Here are a few ideas:

1. **Say "thank you":** Expressing gratitude can be as simple as saying "thank you." Let the person know that you appreciate what they have done for you or how they have impacted your life.

2. **Write a thank-you note:** A handwritten note is a meaningful and personal way to express your gratitude. Take the time to write a heartfelt message that details how the person has impacted your life.

3. **Give a small gift:** A small gift, such as a bouquet of flowers, a thoughtful book, or a gift card to their favorite store, can be a nice way to show your appreciation.

4. **Spend quality time together:** Sometimes, the best way to express gratitude is by simply spending time with the person. Plan a fun activity or outing that you can enjoy together.

5. **Publicly acknowledge them:** If the person has done something truly exceptional, consider publicly acknowledging them. For example, you could give them a shoutout on social media or mention them in a speech.

6. **Offer to help:** If the person is going through a difficult time, offering to help can be a meaningful way to show your gratitude. Whether it's running errands, cooking them a meal, or just lending an ear, your help will be appreciated.

Remember, expressing gratitude doesn't have to be a grand gesture. Even a small act of kindness can go a long way in making someone feel appreciated and valued. As the great poet Maya Angelou wrote, "I've learned that people will forget what you said, people will forget what you did, but people will never forget how you made them feel."

FIND JOY

"Breathe. Let go.
And remind yourself that this very moment
is the only one you know you have for sure."
—OPRAH WINFREY

Many of us who are searching for more happiness and fulfillment in our lives may find it challenging to stay present in the moment. One major reason for this is the constant use of smartphones.

Photographs and memories are wonderful things, but not if they pull you out of the present moment and into the past. The old images and messages that pop up on your phone can trigger you to think about what *could* have or *should* have been. They can make you think that the "good old days" were so much better than your life right now. Whether that's true or not, that thought can keep you from focusing on the one thing you can influence: the present moment. The key to remember is that true joy and fulfillment can be found by being fully present and engaged in the here and now.

It's only in the present moment that you can create a feeling of gratitude that leads you to living your best life.

If it's not the pull of the past that takes you away from feeling grateful, it might be the push toward the future. Although it's important to have goals, dreams, and a destination you hope to reach, they should never come at the expense of missing out on your life right now.

I made that mistake early in my career when I started my business as an inspirational speaker. I was so focused on getting the next engagement or being invited to the next big conference that I was not truly appreciating what I was achieving and doing at that time. Instead of celebrating all the abundance in my life, I was thinking about what was missing and how "someday" I would be successful. Too much time thinking about the future caused me to feel that I wasn't doing enough and that I was missing out on something. As I started to practice being more present and grateful for what I was experiencing and accomplishing, those feelings were replaced with feelings of confidence, happiness, and peace.

One exercise I use to achieve those feelings is mindfulness meditation, which can be likened to adjusting your compass and focusing on the present moment, regardless of the stormy waters around you. Practicing mindfulness meditation regularly can help you develop a greater sense of presence and gratitude in your daily life.

Gratitude journaling is another strategy I've used to help me be more present and appreciative. Just as sailors log their journeys, I take a few minutes each day to write down things I am grateful for. This can be as simple as a warm cup of coffee or a kind gesture from a friend. By actively seeking out things to be grateful for, you can train your mind to focus more on the positive aspects of your life, much like how a captain would steer the ship toward a safe harbor.

I also started to take the time to become more present and aware of my surroundings. I began by taking a few minutes each day to really focus on what I could see, hear, feel, taste, and smell around me. This can help you appreciate the beauty of the journey rather than just focusing on the destination.

Finally, I started to limit my use of technology and take breaks from my phone, computer, and other devices. Taking breaks from technology is like lowering the anchor and taking a breather. By disconnecting from technology, you can become more present in the moment and more aware of your surroundings, just as sailors need to be alert to their surroundings to avoid dangers at sea.

Remember, being present and grateful is a skill that takes practice. By incorporating strategies and techniques into your daily routine, you can develop a greater sense of presence and gratitude in your life and navigate the seas of life more smoothly.

SEE THE GOOD

"Nothing is more honorable than a grateful heart."
—LUCIUS ANNAEUS SENECA

Have you watched the news lately? It's easy to get lost in the negativity and despair of the world around us, but it's important to remember that you have a choice. You can choose to focus on the bad or you can choose to find the good. It may seem impossible to be grateful in the face of all the terrible things happening, but that's precisely when gratitude becomes even more important. By focusing on the good, you can shift your perspective and find hope even in the darkest of times.

Yes, life is full of challenges and obstacles, but it's how you respond to those challenges that defines you. If you choose to complain and focus on what's *not* working, you'll only spiral further into negativity and despair. But if you choose to find the good and be grateful for what you do have, you'll find yourself empowered to overcome any obstacle.

So don't give in to the negativity. Choose gratitude. Choose to see the good in the world around you. It's not always easy, but it's always worth it. And remember, your view of the world is a reflection of your choices. Choose to see abundance and positivity and you'll find that the world around you starts to reflect that back.

Are you ready to make a positive change in your life? Then it's time to start practicing gratitude. Every night before you go to bed, take a few moments to reflect on your day and think about what you're grateful for. It could be something as simple as a beautiful sunset or a kind word from a stranger, or it could be something more significant, like a promotion at work or a new relationship.

By focusing on what you're grateful for, you're rewiring your brain to see the good in every situation. You're training yourself to look for the positives rather than dwelling on the negatives. And that's a powerful habit to develop, because it sets you up for success. Another great way to bring more gratitude into your life is by keeping a gratitude journal. Take a few minutes every morning to write down the things you're grateful for. It doesn't have to be an extensive list—even one or two things is enough. By starting your day with gratitude, you're setting yourself up for a positive and productive day.

A student expressed gratitude to me for reminding them to appreciate the things they often overlook in life. "I appreciate your reminder to be grateful for things that we often take for granted. It's easy to put one foot in front of the other without realizing how lucky we are to have two feet, two shoes on our feet, and a floor beneath our feet. I keep a tiny green book in which I list things I am thankful for. Although I haven't written in it recently, I will be digging it out tonight. Because being grateful starts with me."

Inspired by the desire to create more gratitude and appreciation within her family, one of my friends took action by having each member write down what they appreciated about one another and their lives on pieces of paper. These gratitude notes were collected and placed in a large jar on the kitchen table. Every day, a family member would randomly select a note and read it aloud. The impact of this simple yet powerful exercise was remarkable. It brought the family closer together, fostering an environment of compassion, kindness, and love. By taking a proactive step toward gratitude, my friend was able to create a positive and uplifting atmosphere in her home.

Just as a lighthouse guides ships to safety in the midst of a storm, so too can gratitude guide you to a more fulfilling and joyful life, even in the midst of chaos and uncertainty. Like a captain navigating through the rough waters of life, it's important to stay true to your inner compass and values. Cultivating a daily practice of gratitude can help you steer your ship toward a brighter future and keep you focused on the positive aspects of your life, even when the waves are high.

Remember, gratitude is not a one-time feeling or action, but rather a daily practice that requires ongoing attention and effort to maintain. Just as a sailor must check their compass regularly to stay on course, so too you must bring attention to your gratitude practice every day.

By making the effort to find gratitude in the little things, celebrating your accomplishments, and expressing appreciation toward others, you can shine your own unique light and make a positive impact on the world around you.

So let the power of gratitude guide you toward a more fulfilling and joyful life. You have the power to steer your ship toward the horizon, and with each passing day, your light shines brighter and brighter. Remember, you are the captain of your own ship, and by cultivating gratitude, you can navigate through any storm and reach your destination with strength and resilience.

MOVING FORWARD
REFLECTION & ACTION

"The only way to live is by accepting each minute as an unrepeatable miracle."

—TARA BRACH

GRATITUDE TAKES PRACTICE: WHAT ARE YOU THANKFUL FOR?

gratitude: the quality or feeling of being grateful or thankful

1. Who are five important people in your life? Call each of them and let them know how much they mean to you.

2. Write a letter to a loved one expressing your appreciation and mail it to them.

3. List 10 things you are grateful for in your life right now and explain why.

4. Describe one of the most beautiful things you have ever seen.

5. What experience/adventure have you had for which you are grateful?

6. Give three examples of how you can be more in the present moment.

7. How do you respond when others show appreciation or gratitude toward you?

8. Share a time when you took someone or something for granted.

9. Which of the five senses is most important to you? Why?

10. What made you smile today?

CONCLUSION

We all want to feel seen and heard. Every person wants to feel appreciated and valued. But in a world where everyone is busy and constantly on the move, it's easy to forget to take the time to show others that they matter. However, when we *do* take the time, it can have a powerful impact on the other person's sense of self-worth and confidence. When you take the time to acknowledge someone's greatness, you not only make that person feel special, you also inspire them to do the same to others. I know, because that's what happened to me when I met just such a person.

Growing up, one of my favorite athletes of all time was the football player Walter Payton. He was one of the greatest running backs in the history of the NFL. Payton played 13 years for the Chicago Bears and only missed one game. He trained tirelessly, often running up hills and through sand to improve his speed and endurance. He also was dedicated to studying game film and scouting his opponents, which gave him a strategic advantage on the field. Payton set many records during his career, including the NFL's all-time rushing record, which he held until 2002. He also was a nine-time Pro Bowler and was inducted into the Pro Football Hall of Fame in 1993.

The NFL named one of its most prestigious honors after him: the Walter Payton Man of the Year Award.

The award is given to the player who has demonstrated outstanding leadership both on and off the field and who has made a significant impact in his community through charitable and volunteer work. Payton wore number 34, and his nickname was Sweetness. They called him that because his moves on the football field were so sweet and his acts of kindness off the field were even sweeter.

I loved watching him play because he would never run out of bounds. He would always turn it back up the field for a couple extra yards. His attitude, work ethic, and determination inspired me to want to do my best.

I always thought about how cool it would be to one day meet Walter Payton.

When I started playing Pop Warner football, guess what number I picked: 34, of course. I used to tape up my cleats like Walter Payton. I wore a towel on the side of my football pants and even had a mouthpiece like Walter Payton. Let me be clear, I was not as fast as Walter Payton.

Fast-forward to my senior year in high school, when I was invited to attend the American Academy of Achievement Conference. Each year, this academy honors and recognizes individuals for outstanding achievement and success in their particular field of work. As I looked at the list of honorees, I saw legendary country singer Johnny Cash, best-selling author Tom Clancy, and Grammy Award–winning jazz musician Wynton Marsalis. Then, there it was: Walter Payton, Super Bowl Champion. A giant smile spread across my face and my eyes lit up with excitement. One of my dreams was going to come true! I was going to meet Walter Payton!

I went to school the next day and enthusiastically told all my friends and teammates that I was going to meet Walter Payton.

One of my friends spoke up and said, "Ed, you know there's no way you're going to meet Walter Payton, right?"

"What do you mean?" I asked.

"Well, there are going to be hundreds of people at that conference," my friend explained. "Do you really think you're going to be able to get close enough to meet him?"

For a moment, I felt a wave of doubt wash over me. Was it true? Would I *really* not be able to meet Walter Payton after all?

But then I reminded myself that if I have a strong-enough desire for something, I will always discover a way to achieve it. I looked my friend in the eye. "Thanks for sharing," I said, "but I *will* meet Walter Payton."

Six weeks later, I was on a plane for the first time in my life to Nashville, Tenn., to the Grand Ole Opry Hotel—one of the largest hotels in North America. The lobby was as big as a football field and even had a waterfall. When I arrived, I started walking around the lobby and asking people, "Excuse me, by any chance have you seen Walter Payton?"

One person answered, "I haven't seen Walter Payton, but I just saw Tony Dorsett, Hall of Fame football player for the Dallas Cowboys."

"Wow, thank you," I said, and I continued to walk around the lobby looking for No. 34. A little while later, a person walked up to me and asked, "Weren't you the one looking for Walter Payton?"

I said, "Yes."

He said, "I saw him a few minutes ago checking in at the front desk."

I quickly thanked him and started walking across the entire lobby to get to the front desk. Once there, I looked around but didn't see him, so I asked the receptionist, "Excuse me. Do you know if Walter Payton just checked in?"

She replied, "I'm sorry sir, but I can't tell you that."

Feeling frustrated but determined, I went all the way to the other end of the lobby and got behind a big plant. I picked up the hotel lobby phone. My hands were shaking a little bit because I knew this might be my *only* chance to meet Walter Payton. I took a deep breath and dialed the front desk.

"Good afternoon, this is the front desk. How can I assist you?" the voice on the other end said.

"Hello," I said in a deep voice, trying to sound like Hall of Famer Tony Dorsett. "This is Tony Dorsett. I'm with the Academy of Achievement and was wondering if you could please connect me to my friend Walter Payton's room. He just checked in a short time ago and I'm trying to meet up with him before the banquet tonight."

There was a short pause and then the hotel receptionist said, "Just one minute, Mr. Dorsett. I'll connect you."

I couldn't believe it! My heart started pounding with excitement and nervousness. After a couple of rings, a person answered the phone, "Hello?"

I asked, "Is this Mr. Payton?"

The reply came back, "Yes."

I then excitedly introduced myself, "Hi, Mr. Payton, my name is Ed Gerety. I'm from Merrimack, N.H. I'm one of the attendees for the Academy's awards banquet tonight. Mr. Payton, I'm such a huge fan of yours and I would do anything to meet you privately one-on-one." Trying to convince him, I went on to explain that we had a lot in common. "I'm retiring from my high school football career and you're retiring from the NFL. I was captain of my team and you were captain of your team. We just won a state championship in football this year, and you won a Super Bowl. Mr. Payton, I'm just a huge fan of yours. Is there any way that I could meet you?"

"Where are you?" he asked.

"I'm in the lobby behind a big plant," I replied.

"Can you meet me now?" he asked.

"Absolutely!"

"Okay, I'm in room 2310."

"Thanks so much, Mr. Payton, I'll be right there." I hung up the phone, grabbed my bag with my football cards, camera, and poster, and, 10 minutes later, I was knocking on his door. The door opened, and there he was, Walter Payton. He had a big smile on his face and his famous KangaROOs logo on his T-shirt. He welcomed me in and introduced me to his wife, Connie. Before I could say anything, he said, "Congratulations."

"For what?" I asked.

"Well, didn't you say on the phone that you won the state championship in football this year?"

I said, "Oh, yeah." And he looked down at my hand and saw my championship ring.

"Can I see it?" he asked.

I took off my sterling silver ring and handed it to him. He looked at it and smiled. Then I quickly asked, "Can I see yours?"

He pulled off his gold Super Bowl ring covered in diamonds. "Wow, Mr. Payton, this is so cool. I can't believe how beautiful and heavy it is." I then shared with him that I couldn't believe that he didn't get a touchdown in the Super Bowl that he played in.

He looked me right in the eye and said, "That's nice of you to say, but remember, it's not about touchdowns, it's about championships." Before I knew it, he was asking me about my family, my goals, and my dreams for the future. He then looked at his wife and asked "Hey, Connie, can we get a picture?"

The next thing I know, I have my arm around Walter Payton, and his arm is around me. She takes the picture, and he signs the football cards and poster. As I got ready to leave, I said, "Thank you so much, Mr. Payton."

He looked at me and said, "No, thank you, Ed, for being such a big fan and for all your support." As I went to walk out of the room, he called, "Hey, Ed, one more thing." He opened his wallet and pulled out a blue business card. "I want you to have this. Here's my contact information and phone numbers. If you ever need anything or if I can help you, please let me know."

"Thanks, Mr. Payton."

I walked out of the room and wasn't sure if what had just happened had really happened.

In my office, in a frame, are the signed football cards and the picture of Walter Payton and me. At the center of it is that blue business card.

Every time I see that card, I'm reminded of how one person took the time to meet with a 17-year-old kid from Merrimack, N.H. He took the time to listen to my story. He took the time to say thank you. And with that blue business card, he took the time to say, "I see you. You matter and I've got your back."

I am often asked if I ever called him. After I went home from the conference, I remember being at the kitchen table with my mom and dad telling them the whole story and then looking at my mom and saying, "You know what? I think I'm going to call Mr. Payton right now." My mom smiled and responded, "Edward, no, you will not. But what you *can* do is write him a thank-you note for taking the time to meet with you and for being so kind."

I wrote him a thank-you note, and about a week later I received a note and another autographed picture from him. That day my mom taught me another special life lesson: the importance of taking the time to say thank you through a handwritten note.

In looking back on that experience, I am reminded that as we navigate the storms of life, it's easy to get lost in our own struggles and forget to be a lighthouse for others. But by taking the time to see and celebrate those around us, we can make a difference in their lives and in our own. Walter Payton reminds us that we all have the power to lift each other up and help each other shine.

~

Are you ready to continue on your amazing journey? Accept the challenge to navigate the unpredictable seas of life with resilience, courage, respect, kindness, and gratitude. Like a lighthouse guiding ships to shore, let these five principles illuminate your path.

Challenge yourself to bounce back from setbacks, learn from experiences, and release negativity. Maintain unwavering determination in the face of obstacles, setting each day up for success to gain clarity and cultivate confidence.

True leadership requires action. Go beyond words to inspire others and stand up for what's right, even amid adversity. Embrace gratitude as your guiding force, steering you towards a fulfilling and joyful life.

Become the captain of your own ship and shine your light!

ABOUT THE AUTHOR

With a career spanning three decades, *Ed Gerety* has delivered his powerful message to audiences in all 50 United States and throughout Canada, positively impacting over 3 million individuals.

As the author of *Combinations: Opening the Door to Student Leadership*, Ed is recognized for his unique ability to connect with the hearts and minds of his audience. In addition, he is the founder and host of the highly regarded podcast 'Parents Navigating the Teen Years,' which addresses crucial issues facing parents and teenagers today. His online multimedia program, 'Stand Up for Your Greatness,' is widely utilized in middle schools and high schools across North America, guiding students to strengthen their leadership skills.

A graduate of the University of New Hampshire, Ed earned his B.A. degree in Communications. During his junior year in college, he started his own business as an inspirational speaker and leadership trainer. He served

on the Board of Directors for the National Speakers Association (NSA) for six years. His expertise has earned him the prestigious Certified Speaking Professional (CSP™) designation, an honor held by less than 10% of speakers in the International Federation of Professional Speakers.

Ed has completed the Boston Marathon three times and earned his 200-hour yoga teacher certification. He resides in New Hampshire on the seacoast with his wife Suzanne, their children Ryan and Shannon, their golden retriever Gracie, two cats named Sugar and Coco, and a bearded dragon named Trevor.

FOR ADDITIONAL RESOURCES AND INFORMATION
ABOUT ED SPEAKING AT YOUR NEXT EVENT,
VISIT: WWW.EDGERETY.COM

NOTES

NOTES